A PARTICULAR FRIENDSHIP

Dirk Bogarde

VIKING

To Molly Daubeny
with gratitude and very much love

VIKING

Published by the Penguin Group
27 Wrights Lane, London W8 5TZ, England
Viking Penguin Inc., 40 West 23rd Street, New York, New York 10010, USA
Penguin Books Australia Ltd, Ringwood, Victoria, Australia
Penguin Books Canada Ltd, 2801 John Street, Markham, Ontario,
Canada L3R 1B4
Penguin Books (NZ) Ltd, 182–190 Wairau Road, Auckland 10, New Zealand

Penguin Books Ltd, Registered Offices: Harmondsworth, Middlesex, England

First published 1989
1 3 5 7 9 10 8 6 4 2

Copyright © Labofilms S.A., 1989

Filmset in Monophoto Garamond

Printed in Great Britain by Butler & Tanner Ltd, Frome and London

A CIP catalogue record for this book is available from the British Library

ISBN 0-670-82976-5

CONTENTS

= AUTHOR'S NOTE =

The reader will quickly become aware that I cannot punctuate. It drove Mrs X, the recipient of these, and many other, letters to distraction, but somehow we stayed on course and she more or less forgave me.

It even got to the point where she used my 'dots' herself. 'I do rather see what you mean,' she wrote. 'They save "face", and effort, and they suggest, very well, hesitations . . . not *just* ignorance. They also save time, in some extraordinary way.' Well: in this volume the 'dots' indicate both 'ignorance' and severe cuts in otherwise very long letters. I have eliminated, as far as I am aware, repetition, some names and anything that I feel was, perhaps, libellous, and most particularly anything that got in the way of a story-line.

Mrs Sally Betts, who has coped with all my work, grew very accustomed to the 'dots'. She has followed them all faithfully and might now be relieved to know that they did not indicate ignorance at all times. Just now and again.

The line-drawings were scribbles hastily done at the end of letters, to give Mrs X a rough idea of things. Nothing more.

LIST OF PLATES

PROLOGUE

'Never explain, never complain.'

I was brought up with those words ringing in my head, but, sadly, this time I have to do a bit of explaining, although I shall not be complaining.

This is an edited version of some of the many letters which I wrote to an unknown woman in America between 1967 and 1972.

We never saw each other (well, she cheated and saw me in a magazine or two) and we never spoke to each other. I don't even know, for certain, what age she was, although in an earlier letter, not published here, she did say that she fell deeply in love with a 'scrumptious steward on the Lusitania when I was ten'. But, I wonder? We both ragged each other in some respects; I twigged fairly soon that she was ill and that the illness was grave. She never told me what it was, and I simply had to add up the clues which were dropped in the years that covered our correspondence. So I wrote to amuse her and to bring some form of lightness into what seemed to me a comfortable, but desperately lonely, existence. Her letters to me were *far* superior to mine, which were ill-written, as you will see, grammatically appalling and a pretty fair mish-mash. But they were primarily meant to entertain, nothing more; and this I believe, and hope, they did.

Someone reading them a short time ago said that it was the first time in his life that he had felt he *must* vote socialist. My arrogance and politics apparently 'got to him', although I am as political as a garden gnome. However, I have felt it wiser not, with hindsight, to alter the letters of one who, in over two decades of living abroad, has had a lot of opinions altered and his life-style greatly changed. I hope for the better. So the letters stand as they were written then: the warts and all. There is nothing that I wish to alter, or should. These were the letters that Mrs X got and so they must remain.

When the time came for me to leave France for my return, permanently, to England, I decided to burn all my diaries, correspondence, and various bits and pieces. This 'book' was discovered, quite by chance, in an office-file, along with two or three letters from Mrs X herself, when I was destroying the office-files of some forty-five years which had been kept by my partner and manager, after his death from cancer in May of last year. I had absolutely no idea that he had kept this copy, or that it was in his files. Rather than send it with the rest of the stuff to the shredder, I read it with some curiosity and decided, perhaps unwisely, to keep it.

So here it is, as compiled in 1978 ... edited by myself rather crudely, and unfinished as a book. But there is nothing left to fill it out; and somehow I think it is just as well. Books of letters can be tiresome, and monotonous ... better to leave well alone. I would like to think that my writing has improved over the years. That was Mrs X's plan for me and I have tried not to disappoint her.

I know that my tolerance has improved, that my 'politics' have *radically* altered, and that the halcyon years on the hill in Provence brought me peace of mind and a wider understanding of the world about me; but that had to be done without Mrs X's wise and caring guidance. She had gone, and I had to go it alone.

For obvious reasons I have omitted some names and

altered others; otherwise the letters are as they were. Spelling, grammar, warts and all.

London
January 1989

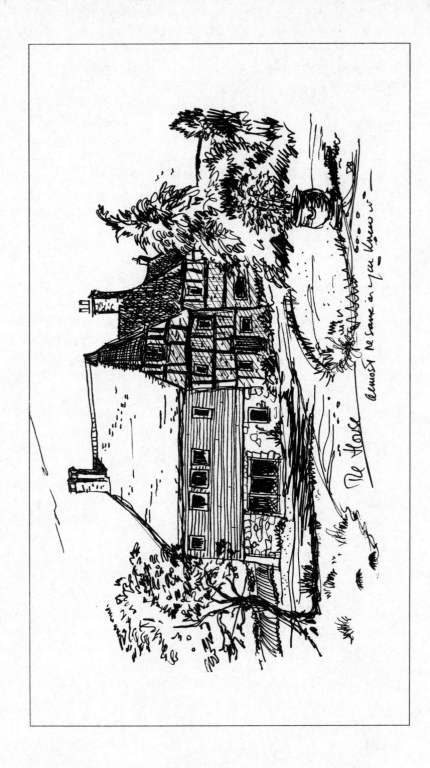

The House

Saturday, 11th March '67

Dear Mrs X,

Thank you so much for your long and charming letter of February 27th enclosing the photographs of the house as it was when you lived here in the thirties. I was tremendously interested, and will reply at length in a day or two, when I shall have a little more time, and hope to be able to answer some of the questions which you ask. Meanwhile excuse this hurried note: I have been away for a time and there is a large back-log to catch up on.

Sincerely,

2

I must admit it is very odd. Well, a coincidence is usually odd I suppose, but this one does seem odder than most you must agree?

As indeed you do in your charming letter, your 'hesitant' letter, as you call it. I was surprised and delighted all at the same time.

I gave the interview ages ago and had really completely forgotten it, as one usually does. It was, among so many, a singularly unmemorable one as most of them are and I remember it only now because you have reminded me. A pale, pudgy youth of about twenty-four I suppose. Starting up the ladder of his chosen profession. Shy (they always are), a thin veneer of aggression, a vague North Country accent overlaid by South London. And having difficulty with his vowels. Boulbe not bulb, revoulve not revolve, pickshure not picture. Unattractive. Damp hands which squashed in the handshake; an over active Adam's apple betraying the over casualness and determination not to be impressed, though what he thought he might be impressed by God alone knows.

The photographer with him, they always bring The Photographer, was older and wiser and bored stiff. Had done it all before, and heard it all before. He drank a deal of tea, played wearily with the dogs, picked his nose and through what he chose to call 'my coffee table books' which they weren't. Really. A bound copy of *Theatre*

6

World for 1933, I seem to remember ... Beardsley ... the collected works of Jane Austen. Too big to fit the shelves in the Study.

And the questions. Oh goodness, the questions. The journalistic clichés which deaden response after the years. Shouldn't there be a Handbook for Journalistic Interviewing? Brought up to date monthly. One replies like a dull child to catechism. How rich was I? Did I mind 'ageing'? (I hadn't thought it was showing all that much.) Why hadn't I got married, how many servants did I have? Did I enjoy being a Sex Symbol? He suggested, tiredly, that his women readers would be interested to know the answers since it was they who had paid for 'all this' ... (a wide wave about the drawing room) I had rather thought that it was myself. No matter. It proves to be The Women Readers, because they pay to see me. As if that gave them the Divine Right or something. Apart from their banality the questions were all asked with a snideness which implied that he already knew all the answers but what was *I* going to say? Snideness is a fast growing commodity in England today. Snideness and spite. I don't recall that we were known for these particular qualities before, but we are now. Fostered heavily by our Socialist Government who work at it hard. There is another word, envy, which has also crept up the scale in popular politics. And that was something we surely never had in our old Imperialist days! For what was there we had not got already to envy? So Envy and Spite and Snideness are the new Three Brass Monkeys. With far less charm.

Anyway: it was that sort of interview, and if I appear, as you most delicately hint, as 'arrogant' that is perhaps how the young man saw me. And my irritation gave him the stone for his catapult. I'm sorry. Sorry that you read the damned thing. And you would have to find it in your hairdresser's! That is the cliché of all time. (Or do you call them Beauty Parlours, Parlors I mean, in your State?) I can't imagine, either, how it got there from England.

But since you live in a university town perhaps some student brought it in? Possible? Some grey girl on an exchange-deal from Bristol or Leeds. Who knows? But inadvertently she set her match to a strange little trail of powder. Of course I can 'appreciate the shock' of you suddenly rifling through the thing and finding pictures of a total stranger sitting about in rooms which once were yours, in a house which you once loved and made your own so long ago. A horrid shock. A film star in your much loved house. I imagine you blushed with anger under the dryer? But I am very happy indeed that you took the trouble to write as you did, or the 'courage' as you call it. It was a great risk, yes I do see that. But here is a speedy answer which I hope will allay, at least, some of the doubts you just rightly entertain from that inter-view. If it is any consolation at all I cherish the house almost as much as you did. I say 'almost' for I have no presumption. How can I know HOW much you loved it? I only know that *I* do and how much. This has gone on far too long. I only wanted to thank you for your 'hesitant' letter and for the photographs of the place as it was in 1935. All gave me infinite pleasure.

============ *3* ============

The House

March 28th '67

No: it really hasn't changed a great deal, the house, since
you were here in '39. Inside at least. Outside, of course,
a lot had gone. The seasons and the War saw to that. But
it still stands very much as it has stood since 1200 and
something and will do so, I hope, for many more years
to come.

I bought it from a fearful woman who looked rather like
a blond wigged pig. She took me round her 'residence', as
she called it, clutching a large Martini and a snorting
Pekinese. The walls were obliterated by a bilious, faux,
damask paper, the rooms jammed with Louis-Any-Kind
and reproduction Queen Anne; barley sugar legs and
yellow varnish. Iron cartwheels hung from the ceilings
stuck around with hideous electric candles in squint red-
flock shades, like blacksmiths' birthday cakes. There was
a wealth (or poverty?) of machine made petit-point cush-
ions and green and beige tapestries of hunting parties, a
telephone in a Sedan chair, porcelain ladies simpering in
crinolines or selling balloons, and wrought iron writhing like the Laocoön from every spare wall space. But
under all this monstrousness, the house was still there.
Brave, stoical, longing to be stripped down and given its
dignity back. And I longed to help. I told her that I would
not be requiring any of the Fixtures and Fittings, and
although I did this most tactfully (because of a third
Martini she was starting to be just the least bit aggressive)

9

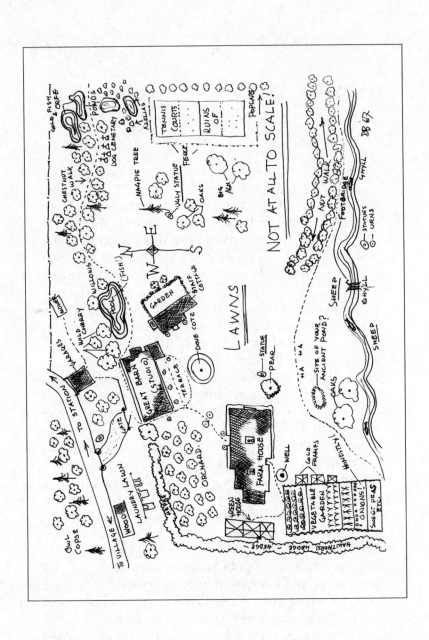

NOT AT ALL TO SCALE!

she sensed a loss of profit. 'What will you give me for all the love I have given the place? What will you pay me for that then? And these ...' She suddenly grabbed a handful of appalling curtains which she claimed had come from 'some Palace in Florence' but couldn't remember the name. 'These go with the house ... you can't refuse these! Specially made for it ... cost a fortune.'

Yes: the Chestnut walk is still there, or here rather. Today a smother of daffodils and narcissi, millions and millions of them it seems. Did you plant them I wonder all those years ago? They have spread deep into the trees and all the way down to the fish-pools in the Azalea Garden. Not yet all fully out, but next week they should be very Wordsworthian if the weather holds.

There are doves still here too in the old dove cote. The Wigged Pig said that if I didn't want them, as Fixtures or Fittings, I would have to call the Pest Officer because she wasn't going to move them. And I took over seven mallard ducks on the carp pond, a Muscovy, and six ordinary white farmyard ones, which she said all had names, one was Dopey, Sneezey, Snoopy etc.: I really didn't bother; and anyway my Mastiff (Candida) got the lot within three weeks. Bitches are very sly. She used to wander up to me, great tail slowly wagging, her face a mask of white down like a huge powder puff: enormously pleased and innocent.

Did you know that Gertrude Jekyll wrote about the gardens in one of her Garden books? Long out of print now. She enormously admired the two little diamond ventilators which were set high in the windows of the old Dairy. Lead, of delicate design, pre-Tudor. Do you remember those I wonder? And did you plant the white lilac in the corner outside the back kitchen? Easily twelve foot high now and burdened in April with fat white trusses. Perhaps it was even there before your time ... its trunk is scaly and green with moss. So many questions! Don't even consider answering them. I could send you some 'snaps' if you cared, to show you what it looks like now after, what is it, goodness me! twenty-seven years. What a rush of time past. More than a generation. I feel, or felt until I wrote that, that I had owned the house for years and years ... not just the very few I have. Anyway no one actually 'owns' a house do they? ... it's merely, for the 'owner', a long lease, or a short one as the case may be: our own frailty sees to that. Think of all the people who have owned this place since 1200 ... as it says on the deeds! You and I were only fragmentary in our staying ... I say 'you and I' because I cannot guess how long I shall be allowed to stay here before Mr Wilson forces me out.

If you ever come to Europe, and I don't know that you do, please let me know. It would be very pleasant if you came down for lunch or something one day. Perhaps, though, not for you? Pleasant I mean. I don't know. Going Back is really to be avoided I think. I did it once, to an old cottage we had lived in years ago as children. A grave mistake. Where the potato patch had been was now a dainty lawn; where the rhubarb had grown, grew a loathsome Laburnum; the front door was glossy prim-rose where ours had been creosoted planks and where the privy had stood in solemn isolation under a great lilac there was an alpine rockery ... and nothing is more out of place than that on the side of a soft Sussex Down. A great mistake to go back. So perhaps you won't ... but the invitation was kindly meant. Thank you for your letter, it was a splendidly swift reply ... Today is my 46th birthday, I couldn't have had a nicer 'present' ...

4

The House

April 15th '67

The silence: of course one is reminded of that here constantly.

Of all the things which might have changed, and have,
over the years, *that* remains. The stillness at night. Not
silence just. Stillness. Lying in bed I can hear the water
bubble and swirl in the long pool down by the croquet
lawn, and the almost constant bleat of lambs in the
meadow beyond. I wonder why they bleat in the dark?
Foxes? Fear? Food? Looking for Mum in the dark I
suppose. London guests staying hate it. Keeps them awake
all night they complain. The bleating in the utter stillness.
I heal with it, as you did.

There is a little owl somewhere. I hear him too on crisp
nights, but haven't as yet found his nest. I rather think
it's in one of the dead elms down by the old tennis courts.
Did you make those? Did you play there often? Forlorn
now and abandoned. The wire rusts and sags, torn in
great holes, the courts scabbed with tufts of fireweed,
ragwort and clumps of glossy nettles which attract the
Admirals and Peacocks, the lead markings buckled and
twisted with the frosts and suns of seasons. Bracken and
bramble proliferate, hip high, and the tall row of Lom-
bardy poplars on the east boundary are as high as steeples,
some are dead, but there are three like Proust's at Martin-
ville ... two quite near, the third a little further off ...
they seem to change places as one walks down through

13

the high rutted banks of the chestnut walk to the ponds. There is nothing I can do now to wrest them back from their wilderness. The courts I mean. Left too long ... since, I suppose, you went. There is a wistful, melancholic atmosphere especially on long summer evenings when the shadows lengthen and the sun begins to slip down behind the trees. I imagine the ghosts of players long past. Not necessarily because they are dead! I suppose I really mean The Shades. The transparency we must leave behind us wherever we have been ... do you know what I mean? Probably not. I am a bad explainer. But on still summer evenings I imagine the 'shades' of players there, long forgotten. But not you ... for you are remembered now! The soft 'Thwack-Thwock' of balls against gut, scrape of tennis shoes on the red grit, echoes in the still trees of 'Love All!' ... Love all. I do. Was it like that once? A bit Scott Fitzgeraldish, girls with bangles and beads, young men in white flannels in low deckchairs: could there have been music perhaps? Layton and Johnson and 'My Blue Heaven' on a portable gramophone? Probably not. It never is as one imagines it to have been, which is why I always get so fearfully confused and irritated in Palaces and Castles ... how can one imagine Darnley or Mary or poor, sad, George III roaming about Windsor, or Anne Boleyn at Hampton Court ... or you on your tennis courts? Never mind. It is not for replying to, promise you.

No: the wild daffodils are almost all gone, picked by the Gyppos you used to see selling them in bunches for a penny a time in the village. All gone. And so have most of the Gyppos ... shoved into caravan-sites or high rise apartments, which will ultimately be their death. Another sign of the Socialist Times ... we must all be neatly arranged now. Tidied up.

God no! I own all the house and acres all to myself. Mr Wilson is our Prime Minister, not, thank God, my Landlord. What a frightful thought. But I do see how you could have been confused. I'll try to be more careful in future, I am apt to forget that you live so far away. And the cold-frames where you grew your Parma violets are still here. Filled, at the moment, with sweet pea seedlings which I am hoping to 'put out' in a week or so, and the lane you ask about is called Alice Sweets Lane ... I looked it up on the map. No idea who she was but someone in the village said she drowned herself in a pond in eighteen something. Probably a poor thieving gyppo who feared death less than transportation to Australia. I don't blame her in the least. I'm boring you ... anyway I am boring myself ... a sure sign to stop. But I was trying to answer some of your questions. You say you came here first in 1932. Seven years is really not enough of 'here' is it? You say, 'With only half an hour's warning we drove to London and I knew that I would never ever see it again ...' But isn't it very strange? For you have, indirectly, after all ...

5

The House

May 8th '67

A strange coincidence this morning. I have been on location for a film in Oxford and Buxton. Don't ever go there. If you *do*, don't stay at the Palace Hotel, and if you are forced to in spite of my warning, don't take the Devonshire Suite which is so depressing and awful that it is actually quite funny. A small one bar electric fire covered in cigarette burns, a crack down one wall into which you could easily insert a hand sideways (I did), and a filthy carpet covered in vomit or beer stains. The English are *marvellous* at Hotels. Anyway, I digress. This morning. So. I've been away for a while and returned to a stack of unopened and unanswered mail. Among the stuff, two fan letters from Russia (!), two letters from you and, this is the strange part, a letter addressed to your husband from the Wine Society! Now that *is* English. I can only assume that in 1939, when you had to leave so hurriedly, he omitted to cancel the order or whatever it is. And it comes regularly I gather from my secretary (No. Don't worry. She does NOT open your mail. Strict orders.) who, not knowing the name, assumed correctly that it was for a past owner of the house. I suppose you won't want me to send it on?

... anyway I'm back. Exhausted of course. It was a stupid, unsatisfying film ... but just not having to rise at five every morning will be a relief. I had an idea that I would go over to Normandy for a bit to 'heal'. France has a very soothing effect on me, to such an extent that I sometimes think I might have been French in an other life. I 'feel' more French than I do English ... but then I am hardly, by blood, English anyway. Spanish–Scots on my mother's side, Dutch–English on my father's. I'm really a frightful muck up. It sometimes gets in the way, I have great pulls and nostalgia for dotty places like Dieppe, Tours, Avignon ... even Boulogne. But I resisted that quite strong temptation after one look at the house glowing in the sun amidst the pear and lilac and thought I'd better get down to the lawns, the bedding out of the sweet-peas who can't wait any longer, and the onions which are smothered in pimpernel and bird's-eye. So, God help it, or me rather, here I am. Instead of Ecrevisse à la nage it is Walls Pork Pie and potato salad. I *know* I'm in England! I sense, although I have read them very quickly, a wistful regret in your letters about your present living place. Do you not care for it, America I mean? I always feel so completely a foreigner there. Far more than I do in Germany, Italy or even Java or India. The first day one steps on to Fifth Avenue, or 42nd Street, or Madison Avenue, anywhere, I am immediately Foreign. And yet one supposedly speaks the same language. (A myth. We don't. But they don't know that yet.) But I am asking questions again.

I got back not only to letters and pear blossom but a Domestic Drama. As usual. The Swiss couple who had come to look after things hadn't, it seems, lifted a finger in the weeks I had been away. Coffee and Kent cigarettes all day. Food all right but a dirty cook, the wife idle and couldn't make a bed! I had to show her how to mitre the bloody corners for God's sake and she couldn't serve artichokes. So I make my own bed, eat Walls pork pie and have sacked them. An elderly couple arrive next week who 'love animals and cook simple English food' but I'll give them a try. How nice it is to have you to write to ... do forgive my spelling ... I dictated the first letter to you

... but now that we seem to be on a correspondence course, and you can pull out whenever you want to ... I'd better type my own. So beware ...

6

The House

May 18th '67

I *am* glad that you are not being bored by my letters, and that they give you pleasure, and I'm not a bit 'shocked' that you are surprised that a film star can write anything at all, apart from his autograph!

Film stars, you know, aren't supposed to be 'bright' at all. And, God knows, I'm not really. I just write to you as it comes out of my head, that's all. And as we share a bond of love for this place, and as you constantly demand replies to your insidious little questions about the gardens and the rooms, I feel compelled to answer. And anyway I like to. Really. But I know perfectly well that as a Film Star, and I so detest the label, I am supposed only to follow the rules laid down for us by the Press and Popular Misconception. Brainless, vain, swilling champagne, gulping caviar and reclining in fur at the back of Rolls-Royces. I confess that I have all these attributes. They suit me very well ... apart from the fur. I have never had fur near me because I don't approve of killing beasts to cover the frailties of the human form. Have you, or did you rather, ever see the women wrapped in leopards all over the lobby of the Hôtel de Paris in Monte Carlo? Prides of leopard cut into pelts to wrap round the ample bodies a-glitter with gold and pearls. I fume. Is it only a pride of lions? What do leopards become I wonder? Packs? Tribes? I don't know. You're the clever one working in your university. I am impressed. Is it all ivy-covered and white stone ... do they wear gowns and mortar boards ... and ride bicycles? Being American, and democratic, probably not. Probably it's blue jeans and Buicks or something. I can never take American education very seriously. They seem to study such odd things. I can't see much virtue in taking a degree in The Contemporary Novel, or Wigwam Building, or Psychiatry or Social Appreciation. But perhaps your university, being so grand, caters for a broader spectrum.

But I do know someone whose son has just gone to Idaho or Iowa or some such place to graduate in 'Survival'. I think part of the course is spent on a desert island somewhere, and another part on a four masted schooner. I suppose if you have no academic qualifications whatsoever it is not a bad idea to be graduated in Survival. With the present world situation it can't be a mistake. Being academic may help you to make The Bomb but I can't see it helping you to prevent someone dropping the bloody thing on your own back garden.

7

The House

May 24th '67

Your splendid letters arrived a couple of days ago, and I have not replied before because of the 'planting out' and weeding and etcetera. Also, and this is a point, I fear I may well become a bore despite your protestations to the contrary.

But you constantly provoke me to write by asking flurries of little questions at the ends of your letters.

First of all, yes, do go and see *Accident*, mostly because it is a marvellous piece of work all round, a brilliant mix of Director [Losey] and Writer [Pinter] and because it cost me four months of blood, sweat and, finally, tears, and tore me asunder so completely that I was utterly exhausted after it was over, and wept sometimes for an hour or more because I, apparently, so missed the man that I think I became. When the film finished and 'Stephen' had to die, as it were, because there was no place for him in my normal life, I was utterly bereft. Isn't it odd? I don't think I shall ever be able to make you understand all this. It's a bit difficult even for me. But, yes, do go and see it if you will. It is a masterpiece of its kind, and it's not 'easy'. You have to work at it, and it can be painful too ... the yearning and the search for lost youth ... the squalor of Male Menopause ... the loneliness among a group of No Longer Young academics in Oxford. Certainly go and see it. It won't be ninety minutes of Doris Day!

But, you do realise, you will automatically break a rule? You will see me. We promised not to see each other, or speak to each other. You will hear me speak. Which is a very cruel advantage. I know nothing of what you look like, nor do I wish to ... I'm not being rude, you know, just keeping faith ... I have never heard your voice nor ever will ... all I know for certain about you is that once you owned this house ... and that isn't such a big deal! But I know 'you' from your letters, and that is the 'you' I cherish. To be fair when, if, you see *Accident* you will not really see 'me' ... you will see me being someone else: I hope. But don't get carried away that the character I play is anything remotely like the man who owns the house you once owned. T'aint so. And I don't smoke a pipe, or drink sherry, or watch cricket matches or wear a gown and tweeds ... and as far as I know I haven't had the change of life. Yet.

Please believe me when I say that I don't mind in the very least that you 'know absolutely nothing about me as an actor'. You really aren't supposed to, are you? I know, for you have said, that you never go to the Cinema and don't read *Movie News* ... and I am all the more grateful that you don't. But I am very happy that you read those god-awful ladies' magazines under the hair thingummy, otherwise you'd not have discovered me at all ... or your old house. So don't, I beg, apologise. I'd far rather you didn't know about the Acting Side of me ... it is not all my life, it doesn't totally consume me, I have space left and right of that for life and living it ... The great majority of my real friends are not actors thankfully, and there are mercifully other things to talk about apart from what the critics said, what your agent failed to do, what your billing was in Glasgow or who is sleeping with whom and who was lousy in the last revival of *Lady Windermere's Fan*. It is all so deadly dull and tedious. In conversations with actors the pronoun 'I' becomes a lethal weapon, much like a club, and wielded as such.

How did I start, you ask. Oh dear! Here goes. At about five, in a blue velvet curtain wearing a hat with a bunch of pheasants' tails. More accurately at sixteen when I went to study art at Chelsea Polytechnic, not far from your beloved Tite Street, under Henry Moore and Graham Sutherland ... to drop a couple of names ... Training to be a Stage Designer to placate my father who had had his eye on me following him into the *Times* as Art Editor, or the Diplomatic. I had plans to act when the chance came. It did, just before the war when I won a scholarship, to all our astonishment, to the Old Vic and was due to start carrying a spear, as we say, the very day that the war broke out ... probably about the same time that you were driving away from here never to return ... anyway no one wanted me for the war at that time, and so I had a year of splendid grandeur, long hair, suede shoes and undiminished conceit as a starting actor in a local Rep company. Went into the Army, was rather poor at it ... suddenly blossomed into an Officer and was a moderate success in Intelligence from Normandy through to Java ... Fate was kind and I landed a theatre job in 1947 and became a 'Star Overnight' and shortly after went into the Cinema, where I have stayed, mercifully, for the last twenty years about ... quite well off, still 'striving' and the happy owner of this house. So there you are. In a not unconceited capsule, that's me. But please, don't let it put you off ... I realise that you have tricked me into using that pronoun I so despise ...

8

No really: I am not 'cleaving to politesse'. That would be absurd. Can you not imagine how lovely it is to have a 'new' friend by Mail? A sort of Sears Roebuck friendship of infinite value, so much so that one is constantly delighted to see your envelopes with the postmark and the by now familiar handwriting ... I always leave your letters until the very last and take them away somewhere quiet to read them without interruptions. What more can I say to convince you? Except that I am not, by nature, a very curious person ... I don't, as you will realise, ask personal questions of you, I accept what I accept, and that's quite enough for me.

The figure I marked on the Garden Map I sent you is actually one of Bacchus. I call him Oscar Wilde because that is exactly who he looks like. He is about 1650–90 I think ... bulgy and quite ugly really. His eyes have a vacant expression and he's stuffing himself with grapes ... even though he was a gift from two beloved friends, Daphne and Xan Fielding, I can't quite bring myself to adore him. So he's got stuck down at the end of the Long Walk waist high in buttercups and sorrel, and rabbits dig at his feet on which Daphne assures me I should pour a libation every Midsummer's Eve. Such a waste of good wine.

Yesterday's news, at lunch time, that the Israelis had gone to war sent a chill of worry through us all ...

the risks of a real confrontation between your 'adopted' country and Russia become more and more possible. And where, in God's name, will that lead to? Today they appear to have come to an agreement that a Cease-Fire is desirable. One hangs in the balance. The way things seem to be going at this moment the Israelis could sweep up to Cairo. Which might not be a bad thing at all for us all ... if things settle down a bit I have to hop over to Paris for a day or two, so you won't hear from me for a bit. Which might be a great relief ... I'll send you a postcard of the Eiffel Tower.

9

The House

June 17th '67

I am acknowledging, by dictation because I have a mass
to deal with, your note of June 7th, in spite of your
request not to do so. Just got back from Paris to find it,
and one of the 10th, waiting for me. Indeed I was delighted
to read the little bit from *Harper's* which you have
enclosed. You ask me if 'under-acclaimed career' is not
a *great* compliment. Well. I honestly don't know. Since
I do not 'push' very much perhaps it is the pattern of
my career anyway! I have never, as far as I know, been
acclaimed for my hay-stacking, or my thatching (rather
good at that, was taught by one of the best thatchers
in East Sussex!) or onion weeding, or fish gutting and
chicken pulling, and book-binding, or carpentry (amaz-
ingly good at rabbit hutches). Perhaps my works are all
a bit too catholic. Jack of all and Master of none. But I
survive.

Paris was fun if you consider taking a god-son (21) to
see it for the first time. Yes. Versailles, Notre Dame, up
all those hellish little steps to the towers, Fouquet's, the
Louvre for that simpering halfwit who is surely pregnant?
and some excellent food at Pré Catalan ... drew the line
at the Eiffel Tower, but then so did he. We went out to
lunch at Ingrid Bergman's ravishing country house at
Choisel, which I think was the biggest thrill since she has
two ravishing daughters and a swimming pool ... I think
that the Mona Lisa, Antoinette, and Quasimodo have all

been blissfully forgotten for the far more fleshy delights, undoubted, of Ingrid Junior and Isabella Rossellini ... one tries ...

10

The House

July 3rd '67

Oh come on now! You must know perfectly well what I meant by 'Sears Roebuck' ... naturally to an American Resident it might appear to be a bit 'cheap and shoddy' as you put it. But to me it was a silly, if you insist, but quite harmless I thought, allusion to a particular friendship of enduring pleasure and delight which I received by mail! How else did it happen for God's sake? Sitting in the Connaught one evening my secretary brought me the week's mail (I was having my London Week), among which was your first letter of February 27th, four pages long and containing the little sepia 'snaps' of the house as it had been. The rest is almost history. And I'll apologise no more. Perhaps I could have chosen a glossier, more fragrant if you like, term but that's what came to mind and machine.

... No, absolutely not. You are quite, quite wrong. I simply hated being a Film Star. For about ten years I was never able to be free. Couldn't walk in a street, had mounted police at Stage Doors, hysterical women hiding in my wardrobes at theatres, one who wandered mournfully about the gardens at night wailing my name and who was in constant danger of being found floating face downwards in the lily pools until I let the dogs loose ... had my flies ripped so often that eventually, in public, I had to have a side zip ... can you imagine anything more humiliating than that? And anyway, apart from all that, I have an absolute horror of being 'looked at'. An eye phobia or something. So I'm in quite the wrong profession obviously. However, if you screw up your gut, paint on the fixed smile, the 'gentle and humble one' (which seems to be the most popular with the Fans), you can manage after a fashion, but it was extremely unpleasant. To be sure there were some quite magic moments I suppose ... but to a twenty-seven year old ex-Army Captain it came as something of a shock. I had not started off as a gauche eighteen year old discovered in a shop or at a gas-station with no experience of anything else than mundanity. It palled. Last month in Paris it was an extremely pleasant, if surprising, experience to hear a polite ripple of applause when I went into Fouquet's for supper, or was walking back to the Lancaster down the Champs Elysées. *Accident* had opened apparently that week ... it was a perfectly delightful feeling. They do things differently there! Of course *Accident* is a different kind of film ... the Fans won't rip my flies for that.

It has been a glorious day here today, hot and still, with no clouds much to speak of. The garden is looking splendid, and smells quite marvellous. The Lemon Mint is lemon, the Winter Savory is spicy and peppery, the big saucer urn stuffed with Granny Pinks, the air about it heavy with the odour of cloves. My parents came over to lunch and later I took them to Sissinghurst. Did you ever know it? Perhaps not because it was still a private place in your day. Now it is, sadly, open to the public ... but it at least means that I am able to see it myself ... and in your day I suppose that it was just starting off under the caring, compassionate and devoted eyes of Vita Sackville-West ... she died, alas, in 1962 and the house and gardens belong to the National Trust. I was anxious for my parents to see the roses before they 'go over' ... it is perfectly beautiful. Mellow tudor bricks, the smell of thyme and the sound of bees droning in and out of the giant white delphiniums in the White Garden ... great trusses of roses roped and looped into the branches of the trees in the orchard ... and poor sad Harold Nicolson sitting silent in a chair under a tree, carpet slippers and a panama hat, the *Times* folded over his knees, watching us strangers clattering and chattering through the ravishing gardens which he and his wife had created for themselves but which, it now turns out, they actually were creating for posterity. It was sad. An old man waiting to die. But at least among things which he loved, remembered, could still see, I presumed, and smell. But now invaded by the proletariat, whom, I feel, he has never really managed to accept or come to terms with during his long life. Americans with those worrying un-finished faces, the blue rinsed hair, the Bermuda Shorts and Pucci shirts, burdened with cameras and note books, snapping away and noting down the Latin names of every plant and shrub ... shrill English women laughing about garlic in the Herb Garden ... 'People Abroad actually put it in bread ... ' and fat, hot women, pushing kiddie-cars with lolling, bloated, babies stuck about with dummies or lollipops ... the husbands in khaki shorts and Airtex shirts puffing grumpily among the phlox and verbena ... we really didn't enjoy it that much, and after a while went away. My father was acutely embarrassed for Nicolson. I knew how he felt. Before we left we climbed, fortunately alone, up to the little office in the Tower where she worked. It is open to inspection ... apparently just as she left it ... her books and diaries ... little trinkets from abroad ... a fragment of stone perhaps from Baalbek, a cup from Ceylon, a fossil from the Auvergne ... pictures, faded photographs, dust. But on her desk little bowls of fresh flowers from her famous garden. A feeling of damp, of non-creation, of finality. I hated it rather, and especially having to peer at it all, such private things in such a private place, through the bars of an iron gate. To avoid the pilferers.

I must stop. This has gone on too long ... I promise you I won't stop writing, have no fear, I enjoy 'talking' to you much too much for that. Totally selfish, so don't worry. But, remember, when, if, I start Work again you may have some waits. I can't do much more than work and sleep at that time ... but you won't have been put aside ... even if you are miffed that you came from a Mail Order Catalogue. While we can write, let us. And when we are busy, or tired or something ... let us not worry or have doubts of each other. We have a secure foundation now. Who loved this house more than you? I! Impossible you say ... I'm off before you start to argue ...

The House

July 25th '67

It has been a month of sheer, raving, beauty. The sun has burned down from an azure sky daily: the lawns have turned from green to honey: the onions, and I insist they DO exist, refuse to swell and the heat shimmers over the meadows like molten light. But. The wind changed this morning and low cool clouds came scudding in from the sea and it has now suddenly become dull and dreary and I use that as an excuse to write to you ... instead of doing something far less pleasing, but far more necessary, down among the vegetables and cold-frames.

Yesterday we had guests from America. Friends of friends. He is something to do with Bethlehem Steel and she is very loosely something to do with the Peace Corps. I can't for the life of me imagine what. They were brought down to see a real English House. First trip to Europe. *That* deal. Oh God! The date of its building, 1260, unsettled them deeply. They cracked their heads on my wealth-of-old-oak-beams, exclaimed in amazement at the number of chimneys, the width of the inglenooks, the depth of the well and could not conceive who had 'decorated' it. Eventually I was waiting for them to make a financial offer to take it apart brick by brick and beam by beam and ship it back to San Francisco when fortunately one of my parrots (Annie naturally, who has a foul disposition except with me, whom she loves in a rather sickening way) bit him very badly and the idea dispersed in an hysteria of Band-Aids, Iodine, and swift Martinis. They left before dinner, thankfully. I am tired. Or was yesterday ... just got back from Liverpool where I have been lecturing 300 school children, and answering their questions, about the first world war. Well, my dear, may you ask ... I get asked to do the oddest things.

Found, rumbling about the study, a copy of Alice Toklas' lovely, idiotic, and extremely complicated, cookery book. Bought it in Doubleday's ages ago to read on the flight home. But must have got drunk instead ... for I remember not a word. Not stumbling-drunk. Just 'un-fright drunk'. I detest flying more than almost anything I know. I imagine it is the closest method of travelling steerage today. I'd far rather be like the lady and gentleman in Ford Madox Brown's curious painting, *The Last of England* ... or whatever it is called. The one with cabbages slung about in nets and a storm very clearly brewing half a mile out of Liverpool.

About the Film Star bit. You were right, of course, the Manhood question did become frightful, and all the things which I had been brought up to believe implicitly that a gentleman did not do were ground, or in danger of being, out of me. My eyes, my ears and my lips often revolted.

The women in the wardrobes? Well. Poor demented things. Clerks in dull offices, girls who worked behind counters in Woolworths ... one of them, in Manchester, I discovered by chance while I was changing. She'd got in somehow between the two shows and hid, as they always did, behind the costumes. But she had armed herself with a skinned rabbit's head in a paper bag so that she might the more convincingly disarrange her under garments and cry 'Help!'. There was a Polish lady, about my age, and of great beauty. She was convinced that we had met and had an affair in Germany in 1945 ... and that I was the father of her son. Her psychiatrists had suggested that she, for her own sake, should confront me ... I didn't see her, except from an upper window, and she was led back to a black car by a bored nurse, weeping. Sad and bitter I felt. Sometimes things were quite funny. A woman of about fifty-six in Australia KNOWS that I 'had my way with her' as she calls it, aboard the *Arcadia* in Cabin 123 or whatever, on C Deck, in the Indian Ocean in 1951. So tiresome did her letters become ... she even wrote to my bosses at the Rank Organisation asking them to make me do something about her honour ... that I had to hand the whole thing over to my solicitors who wrote pleasant, if firm, letters. She still writes, and signs herself 'Toots'. Sends photographs. A plump, granny-lady, false teeth of a frightening gleam, hats like meringues. Determined that I must make her 'honest'. She says that the whole situation is ageing her and making her ill. And that the Queen, and Princess Margaret, while visiting her last Cruise Ship, passed her on the deck and the Queen, struck by the sadness of a loyal Australian subject, turned to her sister and said, 'I say Meg! Poor Brenda does look peaky!' None of this is very serious, none of it really mattered, except perhaps to the unfortunates themselves, but I found it infinitely disagreeable and distressing and they were among the many reasons that I did my utmost to stop being a 'Film Star' and try to get back to some honourable work. My latest film, *Our Mother's House*, has been picked to represent Britain in Venice at the Festival in September. That feels MUCH better. *The Servant*, *Accident* and *King and Country* (which is what I was lecturing about at the Philharmonic Hall in Liverpool, as a matter of fact) have been thus honoured. And I feel a great glow of pride that, at last, I am really contributing something to the British Film Industry, especially abroad. To be sure, I don't make very much money, but I do have satisfaction in my work. Which I never had before. And there is a super trip to Venice! All free, I can hardly believe my good fortune. To be *paid* for to go to Venice! Goodness me. What next?

12

The House

August 16th '67

... at your suggestion I went down to the lower meadow the other day with a large fork, spade and hand scythe. To look for the pond you made with your shells and pebbles. I knew about where it was, because of the dip in the grass, but it has, naturally, long since gone. After simply hours of digging and scrabbling about, I apparently had nothing better to do and it was a cloudy cool day! I came across a few lumps of old concrete ... a small shard of blue glass and absolutely nothing else. The rams were vastly curious and butted about sniffing and staring ... but I eventually gave up searching for your past, covered it all up, humped back the grass and docks and nettles, and covered everything in. All gone. I expect it was ploughed ages ago, don't you? I'm beginning to dislike looking back ... a sign of age no doubt. But the present becomes the past so very suddenly after one has passed forty. Do you know what I mean? Well, no, you say ... not really. Well, an example. A sad one. Went yesterday to St Martin-in-the-Fields for a Memorial Service to Vivien Leigh. It just didn't seem possible. Vivien dead. All of us in our black. Although she died in May, yesterday made everything seem so utterly final. Death is, I know. But a service like that, with all the survivors present, underlined it all so dreadfully. Suddenly Vivien was The Past. It was drawing yet another veil across part of one's own life. Although she was not a close friend she was very much a part of my time. I first met her, just after the start of my film career, at a rather grand party given by a Social-Actress we used to call, affectionately, Plannie Annie … she was always arranging people's lives … and had decided that I ought to be Launched socially. All rather trite and silly and nothing I cared about. However, on this evening I was ordered to be in charge of Miss Leigh. I was presented to her (one was never *introduced* to Vivien. Always presented) and told to get her her supper from the enormous buffet-tent at the end of the Highgate garden. I was absolutely petrified. Vivien had that effect if she wished of putting the fear of God into you by her incredibly Royal manner … she was talking to Norman Hartnell and clearly preferred that to my shy mumbles, all of which she obliterated with a vivid flashing smile … anyway I scooped food on to a plate and took it over to her. It appeared, to my horror, as I saw her take the plate with a gracious nod, to be nothing but a handful of gherkins and green olives. At which she looked for a brief second before turning to Mr Hartnell and saying, with the most pathetic smile, 'Sweetie … do you think you could find me just a teeny bit of food … some salmon or chicken? The young man seems to think I'm a dry Martini …' It was not an auspicious start to a friendship … and the next time we met was when I had to go to their dressing room at, I think, the New Theatre … or St James's, I can't remember now. It was between the shows, she lay elegantly on a long Récamier couch, a small table beside her with a slim fluted glass vase containing one perfect rose, Olivier was dressed in an enormous dressing-gown thing which exactly matched the wallpaper. Which it should have done, being made of the same damask. They were considering, quite idiotically, me to play opposite her in *A Streetcar Named Desire* … She smiled her little cat smile and made a little moue with her lips … 'We met before didn't we?' she said.

'Yes. Years ago. At Adrian's in Highgate. She thought that I should break into Society.'

The cat's smile grew whiter. 'And did you?' she asked with sweet, cutting, innocence.

But later, as time went on, she used to come to tea, and I was invited to Notley, the ravishing house they had near Thame ... tremendously formal and one was forced to dress for dinner, even on Sunday ... which I always refused to do, I look like a Maltese waiter in a dinner jacket alas, and wore a dark suit instead. It was a sign of her acceptance, finally, of one that this was permitted. After the divorce she was desperately sad and lost ... and one grew closer to her in her sudden isolation. I found her a very pretty little mill house called Tickeridge Mill into which she moved and decorated with her usual perfect taste ... it was as pretty as a Doll's House and she really did seem to love it. She was a very enthusiastic gardener ... we exchanged roses ... the old musk ones like Rose de Meux, Belle de Crécy and so on ... and she gave me two one day with justifiable pride ... one called after herself and the other, of a rather violent scarlet, called Super Star. We both agreed, with due modesty, that it also was named after her. A pleasant conceit which she accepted with delight. The last time we met was in April, she was planning an extension to the water garden at the Mill ... John Gielgud was staying, and her pretty mother ... she was happy, but restless ... not quite finding it possible, however hard she tried, to accept the loss of her old world and adjust to the new world about her which she increasingly found vulgar, shrill and ugly. And with reason. We discussed, over Lemon tea, the idea that perhaps she and I might do a revival of *A Month in the Country* with John directing ... for Television! I was immensely shocked.

The very thought of Vivien on Television appalled me. Joining the world of mediocrity she so detested. But she felt she'd not be able now to sustain a long run in the theatre ... I felt miserable when I drove away. I couldn't really put a finger on it, the cause of my sadness, she had looked as beautiful as ever, was funny and witty and gay ... but there was a deep running stream of unhappiness hidden beneath the vivid surface.

And then when she was ill ... not seriously we thought ... I wrote and said I'd not come to see her until she was really stronger and 'receiving' again. A postcard arrived one morning, a sepia photograph of Lily Elsie in a huge feather hat. 'Do come and see me. Do. Do. Do. I "receive" every day in a pretty hat just like this; it looks delicious in bed.' An hour later I was told that she had died in the night. But until yesterday I couldn't, or I wouldn't, take it in.

She had, as someone said yesterday, a bloody good 'House'. Everyone was there, from the most illustrious to the humblest ... and the pale, wan fans, in the public galleries. Mozart, Handel, a glorious hymn of Bunyan's 'To Be A Pilgrim', the address, of great beauty and dignity and love, by Gielgud ... Emyln Williams read Donne's 'Of the Progresse of the Soule' and finally Lady Redgrave [Rachel Kempson] spoke some enchanting lines of Francis of Assisi ... do you know them? They were in a book found open on her bed, marked in pencil.

> Grant that I may not so much
> seek to be consoled as to console;
> to be understood as to understand;
> to be loved as to love;
> For it is in the giving that we receive;
> it is in the pardoning that we are pardoned;
> and it is in the dying that we are born
> to eternal life.

As I said, a sad, but somehow deeply uplifting day, and loving. We were all there to 'send her off' so to speak, and we did it with love and pride, respect and gratitude

... gratitude for her beauty, her grace, her wit, her courage and, ultimately, her friendship.

The Mill is empty now and already thieves have broken in and stolen idiot things ... a jar of her face cream, a bowl of junk jewellery she kept on her dressing table ... three bottles of beer. Odious people. Souvenirs I suppose. Seeing the Memorial Programme one knew that inevitably she had gone. Just 'Vivien Leigh' in neat black letters, a fine rain falling in Trafalgar Square, pigeons wheeling above a dense, silent, crowd ... the soft organ and the whispering, shuffling, feet of us, her late friends. So bloody final. Complete. Done. Wretchedly early, this harvest ... there was so much time left ... what in God's name is fifty-three?

13

Golly! It is a bit daunting to discover that all my letters
to you are neatly 'filed away somewhere' in your elegant,
belly windowed house under the chestnut tree. But why?
I mean why keep the things? I don't mind of course.
Can't, can I? Once they are in your hands they become
your property I suppose to do as you see fit with them.
But, honestly, they are written just as they come, you
know. I don't really consider. Perhaps not quite enough.
Therefore it is a little worrying to think that you rifle
through them on a wet evening and fly into typescript the
very next morning attacking me for 'arrogance' about
some remark I made about actors months ago! I can't
even remember what I said, woman. And I don't do
carbons.

I don't think I said that I H A T E D actors, did I? Can't
be true. I don't. I do, on the other hand, find many of
them tedious and neurotic. But then I expect that I am also.
And there are super-glorious creatures who are actors,
of course. Never said not. Ashcroft, Evans, Gielgud,
Richardson, Olivier, Guinness ... oh, and more. But they
are the Top Echelon. Quite different. There is a Second
Echelon, who are altogether different ... but pretty irritating none the less, and then we have the New Wave
Actors ... the ones who are presently very fashionable
because they are violently anti-Establishment (until they
get the taste for high living and then they join the mob,

40

like Labour politicians) and hug their heritage of the coal mine, the herring port, the race track or the railway-yards to their chests and speak with the accents of the North, or anyway, the provinces. It's all right until they are asked to do Congreve, Sheridan, Shaw or even Coward ... Shakespeare they feel they can cope with because he wrote about Ordinary Men as often as he wrote about Kings and Queens and Dukes and so on ... but when this vogue for the Uglies passes, as soon it will ... well, in about a decade ... they'll be pretty lost. Unless they stick to Brecht or Wesker or those snarling plays of Osborne and Albee. And apart from Brecht, *they* won't last long either. You should hear *Hamlet* in the flat accents of South London ... or Derbyshire. Then there is the Social-Actor. Very busy with the Spastics, the Poor of Africa, Old People's Homes; Good Causes which will bring them inevitably towards their Knighthoods. They work dreadfully hard at this part of their profession, if that is what it can be called, and really do deserve the sword on their shoulders for effort, if for nothing else. The Social-Actor really doesn't work very hard at his Craft. Acting is almost the secondary item. It enables him to get the loot to buy his house in Sunningdale, send his kids to Harrow or Eton, a place in the Royal Enclosure, if he is VERY careful, and invited to those cosy little parties at No. 10 which Mr Wilson sometimes gives, and once there the long walk down the red carpet can't be far behind. If that sounds arrogant, as you imply, then I can't help it. At present there is a trinity snuffling round the edges of the Royals. They are vulgarly known as The Brownies in the profession for obvious, and rather disgusting, reasons. Like ferrets in a warren they sniff and push and palpitate in and out until only the soles of their boots can be seen. Hence their rude collective name. We all rather pray that HM will slap them with her sword and put us, and them, out of misery. All simply busting to be Knighted. God alone knows why; there is precious little reason. Every time the

Honours List appears, there is a frantic huddling for weeks before: are they, or are they not, to be tapped on the shoulder? *Quite* potty. I think that the only actors who deserved a Knighthood were Olivier, Richardson, Gielgud* for the tremendous service they did for their country in the Theatre during the war ... Gielgud literally re-introduced Shakespeare to London after decades. They are the 'caring' actors. Oh! And Gladys Cooper is a Dame. And that's fine too ... when you consider what S H E did years ago for the Theatre it is almost a bit late. I have just realised that I did an appeal, the third, on Television for thalidomide children ... I must be careful, mustn't I? I might get the M B E if I can hustle up a half a dozen more.

I feel a bit gloomy today. I am involved with a film project to be made on location in Budapest, of all places, in October. My heart quails at the idea of having to spend the autumn and winter away from here. Just when I should be getting the borders ready for spring. And I rather hate the subject. Perhaps you know it already? An American book. Bernard Malamud's *The Fixer* ... full of juicy prose about the Jewish problems in Czarist Russia. I can't see that filling the seats, can you? However, every time I say no, politely, they offer more money, and have even said I can take my personal Stand-In with me, car and chauffeur, vast expenses, etc., etc. ... Well. Trouble is I *do* want to re-build the kitchens here. Too small now. And one thing and another. But the script, the dialogue to be exact, is frightful. Not Malamud's. Why, when they have spent so much money on a book, must they re-write the author's dialogue? God knows. It happens constantly and it never works. The director, whose work I don't greatly admire, comes tomorrow for lunch, to 'persuade' me ... We'll see what happens.

To add to my depression, as if that was not enough (I hate being persuaded) the Chinese have gone and burned

*Sir Alec Guinness received his knighthood for a personal service to H M the Queen. D.B.

down the British Embassy in Peking, hell bent on an extension to Revolution. Why won't people realise that revolution never goes forward really, only backwards? Bombs and atrocities in Aden, the Congo a river of blood, and Vietnam heaving and writhing in agony. The world is getting so awful that a perfect, golden, summer day, like today, in a lovely, calm English garden is a rare and very wonderful thing. It is. I should be grateful. One day I shall miss all this most dreadfully ... you were right to prick me for 'arrogance' I suppose. Spoiled I am ...

14

A great to-do and hustle and bustle. You'd think I was leaving for Afghanistan instead of Venice. Going by boat and train now, I detest the flying bit as you know, and boat and train is the only correct way to arrive in that city. So Victoria at 3.30 tomorrow for the Orient Express ... well, it doesn't go to Venice this time ... did it ever? So we change in Milan. Then trundle-trundle until five-thirty the next afternoon. A long haul, but I look forward to it greatly. Not being able to be 'got at' for almost 24 hours is pretty good. There are books to read, among them Nicolson's *Journey to Java* which I have read before and liked better than most of his work ... and the recent Sissinghurst visits prodded me to re-read him, then wine to drink, meals-to-wobble-along-corridors-rattling-through-France-to-eat, sleep to catch in cool sheeted Wagons-Lits with a little plush place for one's pocket watch, and then those absurd golden doors to push through on to the Canal. Always a moment of magic for me. Then the Gritti. The most beautifully sited hotel, surely, in the world? ... from the side window of the suite, across the alley where the gondoliers sit about waiting for custom, there is a tall ochre house, and on the roof, stuck crookedly over the vermilion tiles, there is a roof garden which I have long coveted. Some old poles, petrol tins full of oleanders, roses, and a vine, a trellis of Morning Glories. Usually, year after year, an elderly

gentleman sits in the shade up there with his wife, I
presume. She crochets, he reads. We wave at each other.
'Buongiorno! buona sera!' Nods and little bows. They can
have no idea who I am, it is merely polite manners, like
all the Venetians. Occasionally they lower a rope to the
alley below, and a small child fills the basket with all kinds
of goods. The newspaper, milk, bread, crimson pomodori,
amber grapes ... and once a hen, looking flustered, as
well she might, got hauled slowly up to the little window
just under the roof-garden. This must be the kitchen,
because glorious odours waft out into the still air: basil,
bay, oil, cumin, drifting and loitering among the screaming swifts skimming above the tumbled roofs in the opal
light of the city.

I shall look forward to that all the way from Calais.

I must be off. Oh. One more thing. The House is now
the proud possessor of a very attractive Picasso lithograph.
Signed yet. A view of Antibes or somewhere. Louvered
windows, palms, deck chairs, light. Such light! I couldn't
afford it, and shouldn't have bought it ... but there was
just one place I knew it had to go. Understand? How
could this be a flirtation if I buy presents for the place of
such cost and beauty! It's you who are daft: not I!

15

The House

September 9th '67

Your sad, worried letter arrived the morning I was leaving. So I could only send you a postcard from Venice to acknowledge it. I'm miserable for you stuck in the middle of Black Riots. Of *course* you must hate it, and be afraid, I know the feeling very well. I was in Java during their ruddy Civil War and it was much the same as your experience. The firing in the dark, sudden shouts, muffled explosions, fire and tension. Every creak or crack had to be an assassin. And fire at night is the most terrifying experience. However, I was a soldier at the time; supposed to be brave about those things. How much worse for a lady on her own in a neat suburban street ... Things appear to have calmed down a little I gather, the heat has run out of the summer, I can only pray you are more settled and calm.

Venice is still there. No great change, surprisingly, since the flood of last November. A muddy oil line about five feet high along every building and wall ... but outwardly at least the damage appears not to have been too great, it was not as dreadful as Florence thankfully.

The sea rose terrifyingly that night, roared into the canal in a great tidal wave hurling gondolas and boats and rubbish and café chairs and things feet into the air, ripping through doors and gates, cascading in cataracts over all the little bridges ... but no one died; there is a rumour that one of the water buses was capsized and all perished, but I can't be sure that this is true, and nothing valuable was lost on account of most of the houses start, as it were, on the second floor. Or is it first? I always get muddled.

Festival was hellish. Fat Orientals who buy and sell films ... too much gold lamé, brocade, and dinner jackets made of that stuff which looks like watered taffeta but is really made of nylon ... hideous women with enormous bee-hive wigs. (American wigs are always dreadful. They have far, far too much hair and look exactly like burdens.) They were all too rich, too bored, too vulgar and totally uncomprehending, as far anyway as our film was concerned. We won nothing but quiet praise, not the sort of film for this sort of Festival it seems. Venice has changed, rather the Festival. It used to be pretty elegant, and had some pretensions to Intellect ... but now ... I did all the usual Press things and Television, which are compulsory ... but managed to get away once or twice in the time.

The journey down was ghastly. Anyway the British side was. Naturally. A perfectly filthy train at Victoria ... grubby attendants ... blocked lavatories ... the nearest one was three coaches away and had no water. Good old Britain. Better from the Gare de Lyon. And there was the Orient. All those names which make the heart beat faster. Lausanne, Milano, Venezia, Trieste, Beograd, Athens, Istanbul ... what is it that makes it so exciting? We had to change at Milan because our coach didn't, for some reason, go on to Venice. Still ... we had a super dinner en route for Paris and the train was clean and sparkling, white table cloths, pink shaded lamps, little pots of carnations ... it was jammed with Flower Children all going somewhere ... covered in guitars, grubby old jeans, bands round their foreheads, beads and brooches, and the girls looking pale and tattered in their grandmothers' Ascot frocks. Or at least that's what they looked like. Goodness! Youth *does* conform. I thought the whole idea was *not* to? The sweet stink of 'pot' and sweat along the corridors was unattractive really. Trouble with travelling in what is called here the High Season is that it is as risky as a car accident. You get involved with such unattractive people. Arrogance again? I'll never live it down. Then Venice. The suite cool and shuttered, flowers everywhere, and ice cooling in a little refrigerator. A new innovation I gather for the Yanks. This one not a bad one ... then out with my companions (I travelled with the director of the film, Jack Clayton, and his ravishing wife Haya) to the golden, late afternoon, city ... sitting in Piazza San Marco listening to the Blue Danube as always from Florian's, buying little bunches of wild cyclamen wrapped in ivy leaves ... sipping Negronis ... the scurry of feet and the definitive whine of the American Female Tourists who were being dragged, uncomprehendingly, across the Drawing Room of Europe with blistered feet and aching backsides after days crossing Europe in buses. It is almost cruelty. And they can't possibly know where they are or what they are looking at. Does anyone ever actually see Leopardi's bronze pedestals from which the great banners fly? Do they notice, in their hordes, the four Tetrarchs in porphyry at the corner of the basilica ... or St Mark on his column? I fear not.

On the morning before we left I went off to buy a little china orange tree in a tub for Gladys Cooper (years ago, in her house in Hollywood, she asked me what she should do with all the oranges on a big tree at the end of her garden. I suggested marmalade. And we had fat jars labelled 'The Other Cooper's Marmalade' and from there on in I called her my Marmalade Aunt. Hence the china tree). Anyway: it is a small shop near the Gritti, packed with lurid Venetian glass, china and pottery ... some lovely, some awful ... all expensive. But everything in the shop is fragile, naturally. Into it, this morning, came a short, fat, lady from Fort Worth, we gathered. Pucci shirt, canary trousers too tight, a petit point handbag on a thin gold chain, the bee-hive wig, and enormous sun

curtain

Starlings?
Swallows?
Swifts?

DB.'67

Venice - Le Pergola - with elderly man reading
"Il Stampa" -

glasses with scarlet frames studded with rhinestones. She looked exactly like a tropical beetle. The husband, hands in linen trousers, silk shirt with initials over a breast as heavy as a woman's, a gut, a camera, a cigar and a bald head. None of this was unusual, save for the fact that she was cracking him in his gut with the petit point handbag and screaming, there is no other word for the noise, 'I want the birdcage, Harry Karovski!' ... a rather nasty porcelain thing with wire bars ... he didn't budge, rode the blows, stoically, cigar with an inch of ash which didn't quiver. We all stood petrified at the far end of the shop as the assault continued. 'Arleen ... Arleen ... ' he said patiently, still with cigar, 'I gave you two thousand bucks yesterday, where's it gone? This stuff's all junk ... they'll gyp you ... you can get the same damn thing in Fort Worth right back home, for less ... ' She belaboured him furiously. 'I don't want the goddamned Fort Worth birdcage, I want this ... I want this very birdcage Harry Karovski ... you get me that right now!'

It continued, and she burst into tears, his cigar dropped ash over his silk gut and he pushed her into the street much to the relief of the owners of the shop who, rightly, feared for every sparkling bit of junk around us. I was thinking of tourniquets most of the time ... when we got outside eventually they were still rowing ... her hair was coming undone, her fat face a ruin ... I heard her say, as we passed, 'Don't you *ever* humiliate me like that again in a store ... don't you *ever* ... '

A sort of *Who's Afraid of Virginia Woolf* in one scene. Sadness.

16

The House

September 29th '67

It is splendid news that you are starting a book of remi-
niscences. Just as I suggested: what would you do without
me? You will be amazed how many little slivers of your
life you will start to dredge up from the forgotten past
once you start. It is the starting which is so difficult. It is
a delightful and invigorating thing to do mentally, a
bit tiring, I have found, physically ... but enormously
rewarding at the same time. I started roughing out a book,
ages ago, about my sister and me as children when we
lived down at Alfriston in the mid-twenties. We had the
Old Rectory at Lullington, rented for, I think, seven
shillings a week ... from '25 to '35 ... a decade of enchantment in absolutely 'real' country with our Nanny-sort-of:
she came to us when she was a girl-guide of fourteen and
stayed with us for years. We couldn't say Nanny so we
called her Lally. And that's her name to this day. We dug
for Roman remains (bits of broken china, old spoons,
flower-pot splinters, and once, to our delighted amazement, we found a quite whole lemonade bottle with a
marble in the neck) ... we believed in ghosts and witches,
followed the binder through the corn, helped with the
'stooking' and the gleaning and caught field mice which
I carried home in my pocket but which usually bit their
way out and dropped into my wellingtons. As I wrote an
amazing number of names came back from the past.
Beattie Fluke, her son Reg Fluke who was my best friend,

Miss Maltravers at the Post Office ... Percy Diplock ...
names I had forgotten completely until I sat down to type
the rough idea. Super memories; most of them, I suppose,
all dust in Alfriston Churchyard ... except Reg who went
down with the *Repulse* off Singapore.

It is a bit sad to see the swallows gathering already for
that long flight to Africa, it is a part of Autumn that I
have grown to hate, a feeling of desolation steals upon
me ... summer is abandoning us ... leaving us to the
harsh mercies of winter. Ice on the puddles, frost on the
lawns, fogs and dreaded snow. But today is a perfect
September day. The morning mists have lifted, the sky is
still and hot, rooks wheel above the tennis courts and
Proust's trees like a handful of charred papers, pears plop
off the old tree by the corner of the Dove Cote ... My
onions ... here we go ... are all up and braided, hanging
in long trusses in the shed along with the shallots. Not a
good crop this year ... not enough rain strangely enough.
Because of this blasted Budapest venture which looms
ahead I have had to plan, in advance, the new border by
the staff cottage ... went down to a nursery near Horsham
and selected the plants I want while they are in bloom
still: well almost. Decided on the oldest plants, with the
ever present help of V. Sackville-West's excellent gardening books ... Tansey, big white marguerites, masses of
Phlox, especially those ones like flannel pyjamas, with a
pink eye, called Graf Zeppelin ... Sedums of all kinds,
Hostas, and Jacob's Ladder and that Victorian thing
which is sometimes called Dutch-man's Trousers ... it is
heart shaped, delicate and very Valentinish. My excellent
brother-in-law, George, who is, conveniently for me, a
Tree Specialist and Garden Consultant, will lay the whole
thing out for me while I am in the land of Goulash and
Violins. I am taking my sister Elizabeth [his wife] with
me. Just for treats. She'll have to fly back on her own,
but looks forward to the car trip out via Vienna ... to
which she has never been. I shall enjoy her company. I

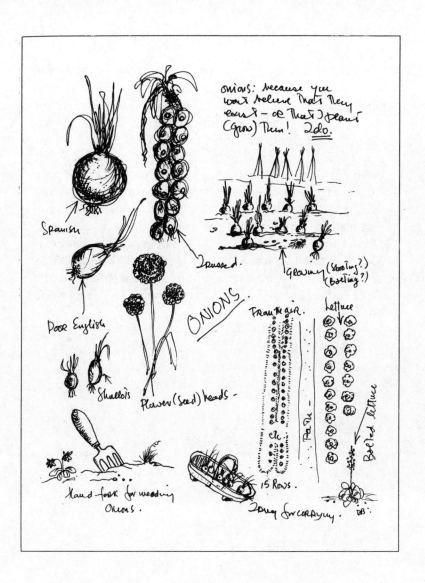

onions: because you won't believe that they exist — or that I plant (grow) them! I do.

Spanish

Trussed.

Growing (shooting?) (bolting?)

Poor English

Shallots

Flower (seed) heads —

ONIONS

From the air.

Lettuce

Path —

Bolted lettuce

Hand-fork for weeding onions.

15 Rows.

Tray for carrying.

DB.

know that the garden border will not look as I imagine it will, they very seldom do! But the anticipation during the long winter is immense . . . and the disappointments very easily managed. Planning in advance has been, I think, a good idea. I don't have many.

I have to go and get passport photographs taken for the Hungarian visas. They insist on them. I have a small part in the film and may not decide to hang about Budapest all the time ... three months is a hell of a time to just hang about behind the Iron Curtain. You need a visa for every exit and every entrance ... they have decided that three will be enough. How the hell do *they* know? Suppose I decide to leave five times in the three months ... what then? Funny world. I am not looking forward to it ... my first instinct was not to do the damned thing. I hate going against first instincts ... they are never wrong. Oh dear! Moan, moan. Just had a thought. I have to plan Christmas now as well ... presumably mine will be spent on the Danube. Would you like to have *Country Life* for a year? Do tell.

17

The House

October 7th '67

I am writing this under a certain amount of pressure. We leave for Budapest on Tuesday by car. Ten o'clock boat to Calais, Paris and the Lancaster that evening, on to Baden-Baden, Salzburg, then Vienna for a couple of days ... so that Elizabeth can have a poke about. Sacher's, I hope! for supper on Friday ... should cross the border about lunchtime on Sunday, and Budapest about tea-time. That's the idea anyway. Busy stacking away the garden chairs, humping pots of basil, geraniums, the precious tarragon, into the greenhouses in case there is a heavy frost before November. And. Bugger it. The elderly couple have decided to give notice. They say it is too lonely and the house too big ... they'll stay until I return in January, but with reluctance. Why tell me now? They have known for weeks that I was going. They have a three roomed cottage, television, radio, all found, and clear £25 a week ... every afternoon and all Thursday too. I'm pissed off and grumpy. I fear that the struggle to live as I do in England is becoming harder and harder under Mr Wilson and his incompetent government. There is not one of them I trust. Nationalising everything from Coal to Railways and nothing nationalised works. I'm all for the working man having fair shares, but not without incentive of some kind. With this government handing out free medicine, social aid, and all the other bits and pieces no one need work at all. And the Unions are growing stronger and stronger and asking for more and more. There is no question that Britain is bent on a slow, determined, bloodless revolution ... but where in God's name will it lead?

How did you manage to miss Gladys Cooper! One of the greatest beauties of her age, I believe that she was actually the very first 'pin up' and her photograph was in many a trench all over Flanders during the First War ... she did all the Lonsdale plays and ran the Playhouse Theatre and one called The Shilling Theatre near Putney Bridge ... she was made a Dame in the last Honours list, and shortly afterwards was invited to dine at Fishmongers Hall, it is an all male affair, the last lady invited was Elizabeth 1st! After the loyal toast, or whatever it was, the Chairman or someone got up and proposed a toast to Gladys before the six hundred guests present. 'To Dame Gladys Cooper. With whom each one of us, at some time or another, has been very much in love!' Gladys said she 'jolly nearly blubbed' but managed not to ... I can't imagine how you 'missed' her as you say. She is as famous as Big Ben and much, much prettier! She is, I suppose, 78–79 now, and still bashing about in a not-very-good play on tour! I once asked her how she managed with the railway trains when she was running the Playhouse. The Southern Line almost runs through the Stage. 'What trains?' she asked. 'Gladys dear, the trains rumbling over the bridge ... what did you do during the Matinees?' 'Oh the trains!' she laughed and waved a dismissing hand. 'Had 'em stopped, dear ... got on to the PM.' And she did too ... all the trains were altered while Gladys 'did' her Matinees ... a forceful, determined, beauty.

Elizabeth has just telephoned, a little anxiously, to say she is planning her 'suitcase' and do they wear evening dress in Budapest. I said probably not ... and she needn't bring one. We won't have time to get to the Opera in Vienna, she'd need one for that ... but you can, alas, dine at Sacher now in almost anything. Providing you wear a

In the Big Room, the House, January 1967 (*David Magnus*)

The dove-cote and house, looking west, July 1967

View from the nut-walk, April 2nd, 1968

Looking east, July 1968 (*Roddy McDowall*)

The long-walk and (centre) the magpie-tree

The House. A Sunday afternoon tea

John Schlesinger and Rex Harrison, 1966

(*Above*) Angelica Houston, 1966 (*Roddy McDowall*)

(*Right*) Jean [Kennedy] Smith and my god-son, Gareth Forwood, June 30th, 1968

(*Left*) My bedroom

(*Below*) The Big Room, where once Mrs X had garaged her car and kept 'a large flock of khaki Campbell ducks', 1967

(*Right*) My 'office' in the gallery of the Big Room

(*Below*) The yellow sittingroom, 1967

Annie, the parrot, and Candida, the English mastiff (*Roddy McDowall*)

tie. She is a little uneasy, I gather, about Budapest. She has a vague feeling that the Russians will be everywhere and that the local inhabitants sit about in dark huts and eat their young. Perhaps they do. We'll see . . .

If you want to write to me, all mail to the Bristol Hotel, Vienna from now on.

Hotel Bristol, Vienna

October 13th '67

Arrived here tea time. Your letter of 7th waiting. Sitting at window marked X. Usual suite (The Chinese!), same old waiters, wine in jug at elbow. Elizabeth ravished so far. Did quick Tourist Trip. Hofburg, Stephens Dom, Kärntnerstrasse, Charles Kirche, Belvedere, etc. Tomorrow Spanish R. School. Budapest Sunday. Dinner now at Sacher. Envious? Hope so.

Hotel Bristol, Vienna

October 14th '67

Panic last night late. I am not to move across border because the Film people have re-drawn my contract. Not in my favour. Furious Solicitors from London, furious Film Company in Budapest. Knew I had made a mistake. Wait until they climb down. It does not auger well. I detest Hollywood. Why did I accept? Bloody kitchens, that's why!

Hotel Bristol, Vienna

October 19th '67

Finally reached Budapest as planned on Sunday. Company climbed down when I threatened to return to England. Did one day's work only, and back here as fast as possible! Hungary is a kind of terrible Sunday. So will commute from here (four and a half hours) when needed. Madness: but Budapest too sad to hang about in. Writing letter later.

18

Hotel Bristol, Vienna

October 27th '67

Bunged off a number of postcards, but fear their fragility, even in envelopes, so will try and fill you in with the details in this letter. Now that you know what my handwriting is like I hope that you will appreciate the typewriter? If you got the postcards you'll know there was a bit of Hollywood blackmail the night we arrived here. Changed the contract, billing, money and expenses. I refused to budge until everything was restored. Finally they gave in and I got to the Location as stipulated. But a very uncomfortable atmosphere everywhere. Why do they behave in this manner? European actors are always treated like shit. Director seemed v. embarrassed, gave me a warm bottle of Dom Pérignon which he'd brought from London as a peace offering. Pleasant thought, but what went before still leaves a sour taste. Never mind.

Budapest very sad. Scarred by the war and the revolution of '56 ... almost no trees in the streets, many cut down for barricades or firewood. Buildings shabby, shellpocked, some gutted still. People, particularly the women, quite smart ... even though the fabric is what we called in the war 'utility'. Very little choice, but they have a great Chic, and make do wonderfully. Goods in the shops in short supply, except in the Tourist Shop in which you can only spend in dollars. Great many Russian uniforms in evidence, not in the City so much as just outside. People are not gay. There is a drabness and resignation everywhere. The failure in '56 has corroded deeply. All the brilliant electric signs have been ripped down ... no free enterprise. The old Ritz a grey office block now, heavily guarded by booted and armed gentlemen who waved us away furiously. Food dull, meat twice a week ... except in the Tourists' Restaurants which are attractive but hideous with Gypsy Music and violins at every table. Which I simply detest! And the food is always served cold on cold plates. Wine OK. If you don't get bored stiff with Bulls Blood and Tokai ... However, the people are charming and warm, and the Hungarian crew at the studio are excellent, and pathetically excited that this film is the very first Hollywood–Hungarian Production. I hope they don't get cheated. The Californian crew unattractive. Met a very pleasant man who was a Count before the war, now a janitor in a block of flats which entitles him to a room. He was very civilised, amusing, and courageous. 'I am the perfect example', he said, 'of the new slogan of which we are all so proud. "We have put the Bottom at the Top, and the Top at the Bottom."' They have too; and it is almost always disaster. You can't turn a boiler maker into a concierge overnight. But they sure as hell have tried. The top Party members, who dine constantly in the Hotel dining room, with their ample wives stuffed into satin and fur and all a-glitter with jewels, look exactly like Nixon. Doubtless with the same ambitions. I don't care for Totalitarianism (can't spell it) and although I am forced to agree that SOME of the ideals of Communism are perfectly valid, like all Faiths it has been debased utterly. The Top Men, from the Pope to Stalin, manipulate the masses to their own ends and for their own power. Why Communism has to be so utterly joyless I cannot imagine. Why so grey? Why so vindictive? Why so terrifyingly humourless? Have you ever known an amusing Communist; or a witty one? Or, least of all ever, a funny one?

Elizabeth enjoyed the trip out to Vienna ... the Klimts

and Schieles at the Belvedere, the horses at the Riding School (we had the Royal Box), the walks in the beech woods in the Wienerwald, but as soon as we got to the border with the wire and the mine fields and the watch towers she sank into a deep depression from which she never, during the short stay, recovered! The whole feeling of Military-ness, of the Russian uniforms, the great barracks outside Tatabanya, the inspection of papers and the almost total stripping down of the car, horrified her. And even though we had interpreters from the Film Company and were met by my marvellous Stand-In, Arnold, who had come out ahead, we had to sit in a small office while they searched every inch of the seats, boot, engine, carpets, and every suitcase. They even went under the car, as if we could have hidden anything there. I suppose we could, come to that. Whisky, gin or brandy ... all unobtainable in Budapest except at the Tourist Shop.

And the city itself, even in October sun, distressed her. The boarded windows, the derelict houses of the bourgeoisie now crammed with 'the workers', the shell pocked buildings, the old women cleaning the tram lines, muffled up in shawls and scarves, feet in old felt boots, the drabness, the lack of lights, the shabby echoing rooms of the Gellért, rather like the Adelphi in Liverpool ... but not as clean. Oh well. It did her good I suppose to see how comfortable she was to be living in the West. Although what she saw disturbed her deeply for she is not fool enough not to realise that this is an advanced form of Socialism which could, quite easily, overwhelm her in her own pleasant house in Rustington one of these days. She cannot understand, and I don't blame her, why a country has to build an immense wall of barbed wire, a wide raked-sand minefield and have watch towers every half a mile or so in order to keep the occupants in 'freedom'. That's what they say Communism is. Freedom for the Workers. But all locked up. Or is it really to keep the corrupting West from stealing in and spreading dissent? That's one opinion ... I wonder if our Trade Union leaders have done this trip ...

POSTCARD

Bristol Hotel, Vienna

November 5th '67

Just in from Budapest (9.30 p.m.) leaving Vienna tomorrow by train for England. Trouble at home. Staff quitting. Must find new lot in five days and then return. Why are you in hospital? Why didn't you say before? Grateful your reassurances, but you do worry a chap. Writing from England soonest possible. Get strong; please! In haste . . .

19

The House

November 9th '67

Well. Here I am back again. Quite unexpectedly. To face
a sullen staff ready and poised to flee. They have had
enough and will not wait until January. Too lonely, too
big. I have done my best to make them comfortable and
happy, even got my long suffering parents to come over
and stay here for a while to keep them from feeling lonely.
My mother has had a sort of little nervous breakdown,
nothing serious at all, but she needs rest and I had the
happy idea, I thought, that she would find it here ... and
also provide company. But not so apparently. Arrived
back to fog, grey light, dust everywhere, plants not
watered, dogs too fat from ill-feeding, even the ashes from
the last fire I had in the drawing room still in the hearth.
I can't imagine what they did all the time I have been
away. My parents have lived in the little yellow study to
'save work'. So many irritations: how to find people in
the few days I have before returning? Tomorrow a Spanish
couple arrive and a pair from Portugal with a child (a
problem). I almost wish I was back in the Bristol pressing
bells for room-service and only having the quite awful
film to bother about. I assure you it, and the dialogue,
take all my energies. Just remembered that I had a box
for tonight for *Bohème* which cost a mint and a deal of
bribery ... forgot, in the rush, to cancel it.
    ... I have sent you a postcard daily, starting with the
first night in Vienna. I hope they reached you? Your first

letter awaited me, the familiar handwriting cheered me immeasurably ... and it was a splendidly 'fat' letter, with a mass to enjoy. But just before leaving your handwritten note from the hospital arrived. What is this? When did it happen? Have you known about it for ages and just not said? Not my business ... but, yes it is a bit ... I worry. 'Only exploratory' you say ... but for what? I gather that nothing 'unpleasant' was discovered and that by this time now you should be back at home, where I shall send this. But how wretched for you. How silly not to have shared it with me ... to be sure I am not exactly next door ... but after the millions of letters and cards exchanged you could have hinted at your fears. I couldn't have done much, I admit, except comfort you. But I would have tried to write a little more than I have done recently ... just so that you had something each morning to divert your mind from the constant strain of uncertainty. I know, a bit, what that is like myself. Not long ago it was thought that I had lung-cancer and got bundled into the Brompton for a week while they did hellish tests and all manner of X-rays and things. Despair and fear compounded. And the rack of uncertainty. Eventually, huddled in a dressing gown, I was cleared. But it was a foul time. I'd bust a trachea or something ... but the wondering and waiting, not to mention the bleeding which always frightens one, was quite wretched. Comfort was constantly needed. So I could have written more ...

Today is dull and foggy again ... the trees almost bare now and the few leaves which remain hang motionless like scarlet bunting from a long forgotten party, forlorn, draggled. Lawns covered with worm casts and squirrels rustle about in the Nut Walk grubbing, or hiding?, the last of the cobnuts. A few roses still down by the greenhouses, but they are quite scentless and cold, their edges blackened by a frost; above the house the hill is mist-covered. It meanders and loiters through the trees, a thin shroud slipping down over the meadows to obliterate the valley. A blackbird is chiselling away, puffed up like a ball of black knitting wool ... I'd better stop this rubbish. Thank you for your letters, and don't please think that I just write to you in reply. I don't. If you notice carefully. I don't *just* reply. I write to you. Try to speak to you. That's all. And it is lovely for me. I enjoy, more than I can tell you, this very silent relationship. I think of you quite often you know; I must tell her about that, or about this, or that remark made or that music heard ... I think that the magic of it all, and it has a kind of magic for me, is that we have never met, nor spoken ... and never will ... what one writes one does not necessarily say ... it would be foolish to shatter something which no one else but you and I can ever have ... or share. Which could be done so easily just by picking up the telephone ...

Get strong, please. Get well from whatever it is ... and try to get on with the memoirs you have promised me you'll do. Not for me. Not that. But for yourself. It will be wonderfully comforting, you'll see.

Delighted, incidentally, that you enjoyed the Rupert Brooke book ... I took a risk in sending it but thought it might amuse you. The photographs, if nothing else, are excellent. I agree with you about it ... but sent it only for nostalgia. Hassall is quite a clever young man, I don't know him, but he is well considered ... you must remember that youth today likes to debunk and he is not as loathsome as Aldington was about wretched Lawrence ... not by a long chalk. If I have time I'll get them to send you 'Chips' Channon's disgusting book. His diaries. Read some of it on the train from Vienna. I do hope that if I ever publish mine, fat chance!, it won't be as nauseating as this. (But mine won't be as interesting either!) I'll send it only because it covers much of the time you lived in Tite Street ... and you just may know some of the 'guests' ... but it is pretty repellent. Snobbish, spiteful, and arrivist ... it may make you laugh, which would be splendid ... if it doesn't make you throw up.

POSTCARD

Hotel Bristol, Vienna

November 24th '67

I must be running out of postcards. Your letters of the
11th and 18th here beside me. What a foul time you are
having. Please get strong now that you are safely at home
again. More disaster at mine! Portuguese (with child *and*
trumpet) quit. My mother went there to recover from N.
breakdown . . . not HAVE one! Sent for Spanish couple
(second choice) who arrive this week. Cross fingers for
them. Don't let them muck you about too much. I always
think they do it to add to their collections. Letter later.

20

Your letter of the 24th reached me safely. You sound stronger. Oh I pray it is so ... don't worry about your 'crabby handwriting' ... I love it. It takes quite a long time to read and sort out which makes the letter all the more fun! Of course you couldn't type lying down, idiot.

I am really very glad that you never saw *Accident* after all ... and don't go, even if you could which you can't, to see *Our Mother's House*. You'd not like it I think ... and anyway, don't go and see me ever. I'd rather be the person you know from these letters, less disillusioning.

You have been re-reading again! Can't remember what I said about 'being' Stephen in *Accident* really ... but, yes, it was hell to be him. And more hell to leave him, and myself with a terrible vacuum. 'After such a terrific dichotomy,' you say, 'how do you know who you are?' I don't know. But I *do* know who I am, so I suppose that is why I can sublimate who I know myself to be to another man's character. That is the total excitement of creating for the cinema. It is more intense than any theatre role would possibly be. The camera lens photographs the 'soul' ... if you can find the 'soul' of the man you are being you don't act at all. You are. Follow me? No. Perhaps not. No one else really does ... save one or two of the super Directors with whom I now manage, by struggle, to work. It can't be said of my present one alas! We are not at all en rapport sadly. He is uneasy with me, spiky, worried

... I can't convince him that the maudlin dialogue is too American-Sentimental and that Malamud's was infinitely better. (He did get the bloody Pulitzer Prize after all!) The whole unhappy film is dreadfully bad ... a sort of *Fiddler on the Roof* done straight. He directs everything as if it was the Holy Bible ... that is to say with spurious reverence. Wears his old combat-jacket. Covered in purple hearts and whatnots, and a huge Lynx Collar (an odd thing to have flown in: one supposes?) And odder still to wear it about a film-set. To impress the Natives I gather. Who aren't at all. I don't think that Americans really know what Truth is. After all they can't even admit that one dies. One 'passes over'. Never dies. Or 'passes on', a worse phrase.

Hotel Bristol, Vienna

December 5th '67

Your letter, and the clippings, have arrived and I have
been called back to Budapest. This time I think I'll stay
there until the Christmas Exodus is over ... I have to
work until the 24th anyway, the main part of my effort.
It's really getting to be a bit of a chore now, this com-
muting from one capital to another. Crossed the border
over twelve times so far ... still the same intense security
check to the car each time. A different set of Border
Guards always. So that they don't get familiar or slack.
Apparently all carefully chosen from the lower echelon of
the Peasant Class so that compassion is not shown: they
care too much for their jobs and dare not show any good
humour. The Russians used the same type of soldier in
the first week of the occupation of Berlin. The thick-
head-peasant who only thought of destroying, raping and
looting. The elite were drafted in only after the first lot
had done their worst. I suppose it is a sensible idea. I have
discovered that *Playboy* neatly stacked on the back seat
works wonders. Each time I come in from Vienna I bring
at least twenty copies of the thing and leave the top one
open at a 'Centre Spread'. We get the car through that
much quicker and the magazines disappear. Good idea. If
you can afford twenty copies of *Playboy* each time. They
sure as hell can't read at the Border. But they know a pair
of tits when they see them. The car has been a tremendous
success here. Apparently it is the first new Rolls to have

come in since the war. I proudly claim it is British, and it is lovingly examined from top to bottom, not just by the Border Guards, but by all and sundry. The workmanship is much applauded and many photographs are taken of the engine, the car itself and the interior. It is also used, with my resigned permission, as a background to wedding photographs! There they stand, she in white with a veil, he in best blue with a white carnation, the aunts and uncles, mother and father, surrounding the car, with the radiator proudly in the centre. Once I opened the door and suggested in sign language that they should sit inside, at the back: great smiles of joy ... and Dad sat in the driving seat. So now we have constant wedding groups in the car park outside the Hotel. Very good public relations. Mr X had a new Ferrari driven down to him from Italy by two engineers. He was immensely pleased with it, and it was a lovely car. Unfortunately he roped it off in the car park with signs in Hungarian and English saying 'Keep Off' which seemed a pity. Istvan, my local driver, was very saddened. However, he explained why it never managed to be started or to run very far when it was. Someone puts sugar in the petrol ... hand across the sea stuff has to be better played than that.

The Epic is dribbling towards its close thank God. It has not been a very happy venture although I have worked as hard as the situation would allow. I have to keep reminding myself that it is a commercial film ... and it has to make money. Not truth. Each time I suggest cutting some of my abysmal dialogue (there is more dialogue in this thing than there is down in a duvet) I am reminded that it has to be understood World Wide. So explain carefully. And it also has to appeal to both Jewish (a large proportion of the American market) and the Christian world. Hence all the Jews in the film are played by 'goys' and the main 'goy' is played by a Jewess! I know it doesn't make sense. But when did Hollywood? The aristocratic figure of the Prince has to be shown as decadent and evil

... symbol of the Czar. To indicate the rottenness of his state (he is dressed, apparently, by Bakst to leap about in *Sheherazade*!) he has two negro youths of great beauty as servants. That gets it all over beautifully. Except we are using two very comely black ladies dressed as boys so that no one is offended. But confused, surely? When I raised my champagne glass, the wedding-variety, not the true 'flute', to him in a scene last week I saw, to my mild astonishment, that it was made of clear plastic and marked 'Pan Am'. I was told to conceal the advertising from the camera. Oh well! Nearly over now.

To answer two of your questions: yes I love Modigliani. Very B I G ones. As you are thinking of leaving me yours in your will I can only assure you that it is not *quite* big enough. Don't be so dotty! Don't even think of doing such a ridiculous thing. And don't even consider wills and so on just because you have been put to bed for a spell. Are you out of your tiny mind? Enough of such rubbish.

Second ... no I don't want the Gourmet Book for Christmas. I'd *hate* it. It is a kind thought but the very word gives me the shakes. And who knows what the Spanish Couple will do with a Gourmet Book anyway; always supposing they are still in the house when I get back ... I always remember, with a shudder of despair, those Gourmet-Dinners I used to be given in Beverly Hills. Deep frozen veal in vomit and mushrooms ... or Alaska King Crab, so filled with icicles that it was like eating a pin-cushion. With the same flavour. Or else things were doused with half a bottle of Chartreuse and burned to cinders before your very eyes by a waiter who was more conjuror than chef. But thanks all the same. I'll be off tomorrow, with the *Playboy*s and some soap and odds and ends for the Hungarian crew. If there is a silence for a few days forgive me ... I have a tough time ahead, winding up my unhappy 'role'. But you'll not have been 'put aside' as you call it. I'm just out of town. You say in this last letter, right down there at the bottom: 'Now comes the leaden interval, after I've posted this: this time there'll be no answer.'

Yes there *will* ... yes, promise you. But not for a day or two ...

POSTCARD

Hotel Royale, Budapest

December 13th '67

Your letter of the 2nd arrived. TYPED! Oh! What
pleasure to see that familiar yellow page after the sad little
sparrow's-scrawl. I am so happy. Have left the Gellért,
some Party Conference. This hotel worse. Look where
the tram stops. Constantly. Will write properly later. Be
strong, obedient, and brave.

22

The House

January 2nd '68

It's all over . . . the long grind in Hungary. The long trip
back through ice and snow and fog, through Bavaria,
Austria, Germany and Belgium . . . and, via a small, and
vile, little boat from Ostend late on Saturday, I drove
back among all those 'hursts', Tice, Hawk, and Wad, to
the House, asleep under a deep blanket of snow, the big
fire blazing with a spluttering beech log, the dogs and cats
howling their delight. I was home at last. And deeply
grateful. It has seemed such a desperately long trip this
time. Partly because of the utter sadness of living, or
staying, behind the Curtain, partly because of the problems
here . . . two sets of Staff quitting . . . my mother's illness
. . . and so on, and also partly because of the unhappiness
on the film itself. Clash of personalities: it can't be helped.
But it hasn't often happened to me and the surprise and
dismay took me aback rather. I have done the best I could
do, experience came to my rescue . . . but it was a sorry
business. The behaviour of the American crew members,
from top to bottom, was pretty frightful. Quite the worst
Ambassadors in so sensitive and wounded a place. Rude,
unfeeling, arrogant . . . the mighty dollar was supreme and
bought anything, they thought, and everything. But it
didn't 'buy' the Parliament [Buildings – to use as a set].
They tried hard enough but were constantly refused permission by the Government. Their fury knew no reason.
'These Commies are broke! And you can't buy them!' was

the cry. Uncomprehending. The individual behaviour to the individual Hungarian working on the film was shocking and ugly. They were, the Property Master from Burbank said, Second Class Citizens. Oh dear! What a chance there was to make a bridge ... how sadly the chance was lost.

I finally left the city, Budapest, on Christmas Eve and drove back to Vienna where Elizabeth and her entire family awaited me! All with 'flu. There. What do you think of that? It all looked so beautiful under the snow as I drove into the city ... Stephans Dom a pale green filigree pencil against the dark sky ... shops, after Budapest, caverns of light and beauty, even the ugly street signs, Osram, Siemens, Odol, Mercedes, Stock Brandy, Café and Bar seemed things of amazing magic after the darkness I had left behind four hours ago.

And then in the hotel, flushed with the bitter night, and with pleasure at the prospect of seeing the family again ... planned and arranged months ago (as I think I told you) ... the Great Treat, I chased up the stairs, too impatient to wait for the lift, into the Chinese Suite to discover my nephew with the plague, my niece with glazed eyes, their father with a roaring temperature and my sister, Elizabeth, with a white face and a tickle in her throat. It was abundantly clear that no one was going to get better immediately at the sight of me: this was a catastrophe. So. Cancel the dinner at Sacher, the Opera, the seats for the Ice Show at the Stadthalle ... cancel *Viktoria und der Hussar* at the Staatsoper ... and summon the Doctor. Many doctors. Well ... there you are. Disaster. Everyone tried to make an effort but it very nearly killed us. They drove home, when strong enough, but not entirely well, to the safety of Sussex. Through fog and ice ... Isn't it always the way though? One goes to great lengths to plan something which, on the face of it, sounds tremendous fun; plan it carefully, at great expense, and then someone sneezes and it's all fall down. It seemed such a splendid idea on the telephone. Christmas in Austria! Lunch in the mountains, maybe see bears; certain to see deer ... maps bought, routes planned, ski clothes sought, woollies collected, animals boarded, money changed, friends to be swanked to ... 'We're spending Christmas in Vienna.' Oh hell! The snow had fallen, the lights sparkled, the suite was filled with great bowls of white cyclamen, a Christmas tree in the corner with lights which flicked on and off at regular intervals and gave Elizabeth a worse headache than she already had ... nothing was right. The best laid plans of mice and uncles fall sadly awry ... No. All right, I promise. I won't worry about you any more. Until the next time. But please let me know next time what is 'up' ... and take great care ... please do.

23

The House

January 9th '68

Now then: I shall be coming to New York for two or three days' work about the 16th of this month. Business and a sort of Publicity Puff for the films I have made for MGM ... *Our Mother's House* ... this recent appalling Hungarian–Hollywood effort and a dull little epic I was making about the time we started this correspondence, *Sebastian.* If I do interviews and plug the things on the television MGM pick up the check, and that's a help at the Plaza. So. You are warned; or are in process of being warned; I shall be in New York but I shall *not* come to your place. Deliberately if you like. We must be quite honest with each other.

You remember the pact we made? Not to see, speak, to each other. I want that to survive, even though, I know too well, the temptation will be hellish ... so near and yet so far but that is the way it must be. I am far more frightened of disappointing you than you could ever be of disappointing me, I assure you. I cherish this bond far too much to risk shattering it. Affairs like this are for the secret places of one's hearts and minds, to be held securely in the private-times. To expose them to the harsh, probing light of normal, ordinary living would be disastrous. They would not survive the brutality of reality. You see: I don't *mind* if you look like the back of a bus, if you have green teeth, three legs, or wear cotton stockings and eat unskinned oranges ... I just don't want to KNOW these things. Equally I do not want you to see that I am going thin, just a bit, on top; that I am not ten feet high, with hips as slim as this, a chest as broad as that, arms as strong as a Viking. I don't want you to SEE that I am just ordinary. Nothing matters more to me than preserving the illusion we have created of an almost perfect relationship and a quite beautiful world which only we know about, and which only we can share. It is ours and ours alone. No one else can imagine it. I don't want that rent asunder, and I know that in your curious heart, you don't want it either. If we met, my dear, we would of necessity meet as strangers. The secure, trusting atmosphere we have so steadily created would be utterly destroyed by the first shy, halting, spoken words; by the banality of First Meeting. Knowing so much about each other and knowing absolutely nothing . . . two quite ordinary people starting from scratch. So there we are. A bit brutal I suppose. Selfish? I give you that . . . but I insist on protecting what we have made together.

And anyway, in spite of all this panicking declaration, I shan't have the time to come to the wilds of your State. After the job I shall fly out to Jamaica. I have never been to the West Indies . . . and may, if there is time and money . . . go on down to Grenada and St Lucia . . . I suddenly crave the sun, and I long to rid myself of the greyness and distress of Budapest. Of mine-fields, of visas, of searches, and Russian faces peering through binoculars from watch towers. I want to exercise my most treasured possession, freedom and the ability to get up and go. When and where I like. It is becoming rarer and rarer as the walls go up in Europe.

Sitting by the fire last night, half a beech tree blazing in the great hearth, a blizzard raging outside, I thought very much of you and felt, suddenly, tremendously close. The scent of the logs burning, of woodsmoke from centuries past . . . soft lamp light gleaming on the backs of my books, old Candida snoring alongside the big leather

Chesterfield, golden flowers of forsythia starring the white fire-lit walls, in a crystal jar ... I read a bit more of Angus Wilson's *No Laughing Matter*, sipped my wine and thought how pleasant it would be if you were there to share. How nice it would be, and how complete it would make it, if you were sitting just across the room at the big desk, your pen scratching away. A time of might-have-been. Seduced by firelight, wine, and blizzard, of being home, that treasured word, after all the impersonal rooms in hotels from Vienna to Oostende. For what it was worth, or what it is worth as you read these words, that moment was a moment shared with you.

Now look here: I have just re-read all that slosh above, and realise that nothing on earth would have made me actually S A Y it to you. Do you follow me? Do you see what I mean? The written word has its own delight depending on the eye and mind of the receiver. The spoken word crushes so often. We have an 'affair of the written word'. Not of looks and glances or nuances of sound. We can not physically touch each other; only in our imaginations ...

It is bitterly cold this morning after the blizzard. I have put quantities of food out for the birds and from this window I can see them scrabbling and quarrelling and shoving about in the packed snow. A big magpie from the lower meadows, tits and robins sharing the same territory in forced harmony for once ... a blackbird and wife, she duller and paler of beak, fluffed up against the chill as if in a shawl, a bullfinch and his two hens ... a ghetto of sparrows ... and on the fringe of this squabbling society, silent, calm, disdainful, patient, glossy feathers, sleek grey caps, eyes black and shining as the top of hat-pins, stand the Ravens. In time they will suddenly launch themselves into the air and scatter the bourgeoisie crowd below in panic, to settle contentedly once again ... and finish off the grub ...

24

The House

January 14th '68

My dear French and British Passport. (How the hell was I to know you possess them both?) I apologise deeply for insulting your adopted countrymen and making your hackles rise. (I thought only cockerels had hackles? Never mind.)

My letter of the 2nd was written, not in anger, but in weariness that's all. You really weren't supposed to take it so seriously. It was a sort of rueful remembering about the unhappiness of the preceding months. Of *course* there are delightful, good, and honourable Americans. I know that, honestly . . . I even know some. Cherished friends as worried and caring about the state of the world as I am. More so. For they are far more literate and aware than I.

But, unhappily, they are not the people who work in the Movies and get sent to Foreign Parts as, more or less, ambassadors for their splendid country. And the people who *are* can cause the most appalling damage to world relations by their ignorance and bias. Of course, oh goodness yes! the same type prevails in Britain. Masses of them. Bigoted, insular, rude and mistrustful. I have seen it constantly with many British film crews in France, Italy, Spain and so on . . . so I don't only blame the Americans. Don't be too angry. I do think it was a perfect muck-up in Budapest. I do think it could have been better handled, I do think dreadful impressions were made by some ignorant louts, and I do think that for such a delicate mission,

82

the first big East–West film since before the war, better
people could have been chosen. Deliberately. But I really
can't lay all the blame on Americans. Or, at least, I didn't
intend to. Sorry.

But more worrying than that, you are still not well. Oh
shit. I promised not to worry ... but now it seems I
must. I am sad too. Sad for you and your mine-fields of
depression and doubt ... they always seem to stretch
before one in this life of ours, however apparently serene,
content and cow-like one becomes ... the little trip-wires
of fear spill one on to them so swiftly. The only good
thing is that they, the mine-fields, are soon passed, *really,*
it is the journey towards them which is so frightful and
bogey-ridden, the wild idiot apprehensions, the fluttering
heart caught like a linnet in a net of despair and terror.
Oh, indeed I know. But once the minefield is literally
ahead and there for one to see, then *somehow or other* one
crosses it and goes over, and suddenly as a mist on a
morning in May ... it is clear and fear lifts and that part
is behind, with hope and repair and courage ahead. And
if your dear frontispiece *is* to be fiddled about with, well
... what can I say? Wretched indeed. But far better that
than those quick and observing eyes, those keen and
delighted ears, that tongue to laugh and to read aloud
with, to taste garlic, and mint, radish and whisky-laced-
tea! Rather those organs of such value were left un-fiddled-
about-with. Rather. Oh much much rather.

I don't suppose that any of this makes much sense, or
gives you cheer ... but it is meant to. You asked me to
put out a hand for comfort in this dark moment ... and
I hope that you have grasped it. All that I have to do is
hold you fast during these next few weeks until you cross
your minefield and they have a room for you in the Clinic
... or whatever it is. And that I shall try my hardest to
do. I suppose that I shall be at the Plaza by the time this
reaches you ... and even though I am certain I shan't have
time to write you letters I shall, on the other hand, swamp

you with postcards ... they will descend on you like a flight of starlings! I'll try for one a day, to keep you informed of my Pilgrim's Progress through what MGM call 'Total Exposure' ... and to confirm the strength of my grasp ...

25

Frenchman's Cove
Jamaica

January 30th '68

If I turn too sharply to the left in my bed and happen to
fall out I'd land in the sea a hundred feet below. Having
first gone through the plate glass window, of course. This
is a lovely hotel. Main house in the middle of wild and
jungly gardens, a scatter of cottages well screened from
each other and far apart, all this above a tiny bay of such
beauty that one's breath is literally caught each time one
sees it. Golden sand, coconut palms, high rocks, lush
Gaugin-plants and flowers, a crystal clear river which runs
swiftly through the sands and spills into the aquamarine
sea: to fuse in a lather of little white-foam covered waves.
The air is heavy with the scent of pimento, hibiscus, and
salt. All in all as near to Paradise as one can get I imagine.
My little house, up here on the very edge of the cliff, is
called Silver Hill. I have a pleasant maid called Norah and
a fine looking butler called Tom. She comes to 'do' the
house, and make breakfast ... a plate piled with pawpaw,
mango, pale green bananas ... scalding coffee. Tom waits
at table on the beach ... where all lunches are taken from
a gigantic buffet set under the palms with ten chefs in
white hats and sparkling aprons ... and at dinner in the
evening in the Main House.

It is an extraordinary existence; one is totally cosseted,
as you may see ... and I lift not a finger save to sip from
my rum-punch (over-rated I think) or turn the pages of
my book ... Dom Pérignon flows from springs, it would

seem, and the cottage has a splendid hi-fi arrangement ...
vast bathroom with a square bath ... which is much less
inhibiting than you might think ... enormous sitting
room with great windows which look out over the tiny
bay across the azure sea to Cuba, about a hundred and
fifty miles away. It is wonderfully calm and peaceful ...
nothing to do after dark falls at about seven except sit and
read or listen to music and drink, what else?, my Dom.
At first the only music was jazz and the Beatles and
Sinatra. But I managed to obtain, from the Manager who is
English and leaning backward to make the place a success,
some Mozart, César Franck, and Beethoven ... no one,
he assured me, had *ever* asked for 'that sort of tape' before.
Judging by the guests on the beach at luncheon it does
not surprise me. Very noisy, very rich, very ugly, very
vulgar. Texans from the north. The women are all about
forty–sixty in little girl broderie anglaise swim suits from
Lord and Taylors or Saks, and huge straw hats from the
local market in Port Antonio; the men all fifty to seventy.
Guts, tits, shaggy white chests, bald, cigars, Bermuda
shorts ... all blind drunk, and very noisy with it, on rum-
punches and enormous Bloody Marys by noon. I have
avoided them all by having Tom secure me an isolated
position right away at the side of the cliff, by the river and
under two giant palms. The sound of the constant Atlantic
surf nearly obliterates the screams and giggles and loud-
common-crow-voices bantering in the sun like school
children. Tom dislikes them all. He pointed out one
woman of about fifty something, who had once been
pretty, in a too tight swimsuit and streaming chiffon
duster-coat. He goes up to her little house some afternoons
for twenty dollars a time. 'She likes all she can git,' he
said sourly, 'and I got two wives an' eight kids and I like
the races, so ...' He shrugged his big shoulders and fixed
his cummerbund (they wear black trousers and black bow
ties on the beach. Each one wears a different coloured
cummerbund so that his 'owner' can distinguish him the

better. On the assumption, I suppose, that all cats are black in the dark or something . . .), and with a slow smile, but anger behind it, he added, 'Jest across there, three hundred miles away, in that Florida . . . she'd call that rape. An' they'd string me up man. But here . . . why she cain't git enough of it.'

Anyway: I stay away from them and only eat in the main house occasionally, and early, while they are all pouring down the Martinis in the bar. It is pleasanter in the cottage, and Norah cooks a marvellous rice dish and does the washing up. And I get on with Colette and *Earthly Paradise* which seems almost too appropriate reading for here . . . and thumb through a couple of scripts, which are sort-of homework. One from Jean Renoir which I like enormously, very simple, Belle Epoque, tender and full of enchantment, especially if directed by him . . . and another which is vastly different . . . a sort of *Macbeth* loosely based on a family like the Krupps . . . Germany in 1932 . . . for a very famous Italian Director called Luchino Visconti. However, as far as I can see (haven't got into it much) . . . it is a bit heavy and the role he wants me for, the Macbeth-sort-of, is pretty dull. I think I'll very likely accept Renoir. It 'feels' better. And I admire him tremendously. But for the moment I am recovering from the New York slaughter . . . and it was . . . and only want to sit in the sea, read, listen to music and occasionally, drive up into the hills and potter about in the little villages with such odd names. Windsor, Reading, Nonsuch, Sherwood Forest; the children swarm about one, like clouds of tiny, brilliant, butterflies. Everyone is friendly. As long as you smile . . . and particularly if you are English. They don't much care for the Americans who haven't quite got the 'touch' it appears. But there are grave problems here, even I can see that. Too much poverty and too much luxury side by side . . . there is nothing in the way of work except to be a waiter or a waitress in the luxury hotels . . . and that leads to deep resentment. Otherwise banana plantations or sugar ... and a new Bauxite mine down south ... but it'll all blow up one day. It is bound to. I'd never think of owning a house here ... much as I have been tempted in the last few days. Some ravishing places and the island is absolutely glorious. But. Not for me. There'll be bad trouble here in a decade or so, maybe earlier ... and Whitey will only have himself to blame. A charming, retired, Priest said the other day in Port Antonio that the main trouble here was population. 'Can't get it into the Jamaican's head that having a bit of bed means children. They can't put sex and babies together at all! So of course, sex being their main occupation, we have a tremendous end-product and it can't be controlled, educated, fed or employed. Of course it'll all end in tears, you'll see ...' Back to New York for a couple of days on the 5th ... then home. Hope you have had my constant stream of starlings? One a day ... so long as they get mailed from here. One can't be sure. I'll take this into the post office in the village and make sure it is stamped correctly.

26

Frenchman's Cove
Jamaica

February 2nd '68

Got back here just before dusk after a superb day on a three mile long beach at Piera ... nothing but miles of silver sand and mangrove, no people, apart from one old shepherd mounted on a rangy horse, and, late in the afternoon, a big fat negress swarmed about with children, who sauntered along the beach with a huge basket on her head filled with every kind of fruit you could imagine. It was a day of unbelievable beauty and solitude. I have never felt so happy and relaxed and lost to the world.

And then, reaching Silver Hill, your letter. That rather shattered the day. Of course I should have realised that you would read your papers! But I am deeply relieved that you did NOT cheat and look at the Television. The two or three programmes I had to do were, to say the least of it, extremely embarrassing, as they always are if you have to 'plug' the bloody goods.

But obviously the interview in *The New York Times* has distressed you. I am sorry. Truly sorry. But yes, yes, yes, I DID say it and I was not misquoted. I have it in my mind to leave England. I said nothing about 'selling up the house' as you know ... read it again if you aren't sure ... I simply said that I saw no future for me in England today and that I might clear off and live abroad where the work seems to be now. There is certainly none, for me at any rate, in my own country. The last two films I have done there were done for American Companies ... the

only offers of work I receive now are from France or Italy
... or from Hollywood. Which I detest. Why should I
then work my ass off in Italy, for example, who offer me
the job and come back to England and have all I have
earned removed in taxes? I have paid and paid. I'd rather
pay the taxes in Italy or France ... they give me the
chance, they should get the tax. Surely that is fair? I have
had many offers from abroad in the last few years, all of
which I have refused on Patriotic grounds, odd as it may
seem, but that doesn't get you far. All I have been asked
to do in England, since 1966, is a bit of dull television
or commentaries for Government documentaries. I have
been a top star there for twenty years. Too long. People
are bored with me now; not the audiences I hasten to
guess, but the people who actually make films. One very
famous producer [Sam Spiegel], when I was suggested to
him recently, said, 'Dirk is a sweet fellow and a very good
actor ... but if I hear his name mentioned just once more
I'll throw up.' Which seemed an ominous sign. And now,
with at least two firm offers of films, both to be made
entirely abroad and taking almost a year to make, I see no
reason to stay on in England. The work is *abroad*.

I know this will shock you, I know that you can't
approve ... but why should I pack up the house for one
year, or even more perhaps, and pay a staff to maintain it,
while I work in another country? I think that at the age I
am now I should make a break and try something new,
accept other challenges and at least *risk*. To be truthful I
am a little weary of the House-Routine. The week-end
parties of ten to twelve people, the rocketing prices, the
constant effort to keep the gardens and rooms in good
shape, the same faces always, the same meals, the same
everything. I have an urge to wander ... to move on. I
have never felt absolutely settled in England. I know it
seems odd to you but that is how it is ... and, another
thing, I detest and distrust the present Government which
is soft, weak, spiteful and hanging on to power by flatter-

ing the Unions and the much-abused Working Class.
People want less and less work and more and more money
... Britain has always, anyway since I was born, been an
apathetic, insular, muddling country. They prided themselves on these vices as if they were virtues. And through
this insularity, greed, and apathy they are willy-nilly being
led into a form of Socialism which can only, one day, lead
to a form of mild Communism which they will discover
too late. And they are the most un-Communist race on
God's earth. But by the time they wake up, with their
Free Medicine, Free Time, Social Securities and all the
goodies they need without any incentive to work for these
things, they'll be trapped. And it'll be too late, because
this is a slow process, this Socialistic climb ... they don't
really know that they are unleashing the genie from the
bottle and that they won't be able to get him back.
Already, even today, a lot of 'little freedoms' are being
quietly abolished: the ordinary man hasn't tumbled to this
... yet. And by the time he does, it'll all have happened
and he'll have lost his precious freedom for generations.
I don't want to be part of this Brave New World. I have
had one war, and all the things I was supposed to be
fighting for then are quite suddenly no longer applicable
today. The meanings have all changed. Democracy can be
anything you care to call it now. It meant something quite
different in 1939, or so it seems to me. All men can not
be equal; all men can not be totally free: you don't need
three months in Hungary to prove this; the fat Party
Members and their pig-faced wives plump in shiny
brocade and platinum mink dining at the Gellért, the old
woman clearing the tram-lines outside in the slush. The
man at Lake Balaton, one day, who had fled in '56 and
returned under an amnesty only to be restricted in per-
petuity to the Lake *without* a work-card. His only possi-
bility of living at all is managing to scratch an existence by
waiting, or washing up, in the summer at the restaurants
around the water. He was resigned. He said his greatest

deprivation really was not being able to get to the city and the British Embassy where he used to read all the newspapers in the library. He was in a complete limbo. I promised to send him the airmail *Times* and took his address ... he did get some copies I gather: at first. When he gave me his address he showed me, with some emotion, a rather crumpled postcard of H M the Queen standing in her coronation robes. It was hidden in the lining of his old wallet ... I have digressed myself. Equal? Free? Perhaps I have a bee in my bonnet. I am not a political person at all. I am only able to 'sense' things, and what I sense is happening in Britain today is not good. Or right. Or safe. We are running down. We keep on saying that it 'couldn't happen here', but it can, and is. The members of the far Left are strongly entrenched and the Government too weak, and too timid, to cope with a Fifth Column which is already very strong within the Party. If I felt that there was anything I could do by staying on I would. But an actor in politics is an absurdity! We are too emotional, too unstable, too mercurial for that! And in any case, I have done my part: I care passionately for the Britain that was: I detest, with an equal passion, the Britain it has become. But the majority are perfectly satisfied, they voted it all in, and it would appear that they are comfortable and happy with it all. And if that is what the majority want, who am I to suggest that they are wrong? Wrong for me. But not wrong for them. Yet.

I'm sorry. I'm belting off. You did provoke it really ... well, perhaps it was not you, but nice Miss Smith of *The New York Times* who did it by asking, perfectly innocently, why I didn't leave and come to America to work ... since there were so few opportunities now left for me in Britain. She sort of, suddenly, crystallised my wandering thoughts, my discontent, and they were gathered together firmly. *Why stay?* But I have little empathy for America, I am English and always will be: but European. And there I'll stay. In Europe. But not, I think, on our Tight Little

Island which is busily disarming itself, overtaking itself, and pouring those taxes into all the nationalised industries which are failing disastrously, instead of supporting a military strength to combat the inevitable enemy in the East. Oh if only they could see what was happening to themselves. It is 1938 all over again ... So my dear the secret, if ever it was a secret, is out. I *shall* think of moving away ... but it very much depends on the work that there is available for me to do. I have little money and I have to work. How strange! The future, as far as I am concerned anyway, depends on two, as yet unknown, men. Renoir and Visconti. They have beckoned ... it would seem, under the present circumstances, foolhardy of me not to follow ...

27

The House

February 13th '68

Your letters of the 8th and 9th have arrived and given me no little measure of relief and gratitude. At least some of your fears are lessened even though the operation still looms. But it isn't cancer and Thank God for that. I'll wait for news. I'll be patient, don't fuss. I am so relieved that I can contain my contentment with pleasure.

Foggy today. The low kind with a grumpy sky above. Mild. Damp. The house dim in the grey light reflected. In the nut walk the daffodils are four inches high already, green furled umbrellas thrusting through the dead grasses. The tulips which I scattered about last autumn in handfuls and wild abandon among the rough under the acacias are, already, slender funnels, dew-filled, standing strong among the first aconites and snowdrops. They promise, but don't yet guarantee, glowing drifts of white and yellow for May. But I am seldom lucky in my garden planning. Far too full of imagination and not enough practicality.

It is so strange to be back here in the soft mist-drifting-hills after the harsh colours and scents of Jamaica. No longer the ting-tong cry of the bright-eyed starlings which sat in the banyan tree over my little river on the beach not so long ago . . . now the muted cooing of the doves, the tender colours of the early wheat, the pale stubble, the pearl light, the trees down in the valley, lace-fans against the drifting, curling, fog wreathing up from the sea. All a change too from the Whore-New York who so beguiles me with her shoddy splendours. How different, reserved, chic even, London was yesterday. And yet ... and yet ... I miss New York. The skyline coming in from Kennedy ... Broadway ... the high buildings on Park, golden diamonds against the plum and saffron of the evening sky. The Plaza, the whole *nonsense* of it! A mock-château with its absurd turrets, cliffs of windows, the clusters of Edwardian lamps, the doormen who know one ... the glittering elevators riding smoothly to the familiar sixth floor ... Mary rushing along the corridor to greet one, face cracked with pleasure, white apron flying ... 'Ah! 'Tis you at last! Knew you was coming ... we're all ready for you, did you have a good trip? Jamaica! Well then, *what* outlandish places ...' Mary has been in America since she was a baby in arms and arrived at what she calls The Island, in 1909. But it only seems like last week. She has never been 'home' since and has a brogue as heavy as a truck driver's. She's been on the Floor at the Plaza for thirty-five years in one capacity or another. 'You'll see changes, mark my words, me dear ... terrible changes. Pop singers now if you please! It's all gone wrong since we had the Jews, we were a restricted hotel in the good old days ... but now ... well ... they'll be letting in the Niggers next thing ... see if I'm right. There's a lot of flowers for you ... the notes are on the desk ... take no notice of the ferns there, they're plastic ...'

And from the window the seducing view right up the Park to the reservoirs, to Harlem, across the skating rink, the lake, the Zoo ... the towers of the Dakota building immense exclamation marks against the fading sun. But the ferns *were* plastic, the suite had been re-decorated since last time. That ugly varnished fake-fruit wood Louis something or other. Scatters of little prints framed in worm-wood and chipped gilt ... porridgy tweed chairs, the obligatory pair of sofa-lamps, Tang Horses this time, with wide drum shades ... and outside the streets were shabby, pot-holed, littered with paper and cigarette packets ... New York is a tease; all the wrong values spring to one's eyes ... Anyway: I spent most of the time in the suite giving my interviews, and that was a funny old week, but for a later letter. I'm only just thawing out, or should it be in? I seem to have been on the run ever since we set off to Budapest oh ... light years ago ...

28

The House

February 22nd '68

... I'm sorry that you got 'muddled' with the things you read in the Press while I was in NY. You MUST realise that I have to live two kinds of life, one public and one private. You have the key to the private one ... but the public one is not so bad, really. I know it is not 'like you' ... why should it be? Indeed how could it be? One has to conform to a certain standard which has been set and which is expected. I couldn't be the person you know with a total stranger from, say, *Newsweek* or *Women's Wear Daily*. How could I? So of course you were muddled. And I know that you were distressed by the *Times* thing, but the very pleasant woman meant no harm, and indeed gave me what we call very good space. And kindly; whatever you may privately feel.

It was a hellish time honestly, Total Exposure always is. It starts with breakfast (for God's sake) at seven forty-five ... and that's no joke. Some quite unknown person shares your boiled egg and asks inane questions. And it goes on until the last appointment, usually at supper somewhere. There isn't time to have a pee really ... although here and there in the fat typed list one is handed on arrival at the airport there is something called 'SC'. It lasts fifteen minutes and means, literally, 'Shirt Change'. The morning is usually spent with the not-very-important Press. They get an exact twenty minutes each. Lunch is an hour and a half and taken with a VIP. Someone from the *Times* or *New York* or *Time* . . . the afternoon is divided into hours with the rather more important people, or Television or Radio or something . . . on up to dinner with someone else, usually planning the events for tomorrow. There isn't even time to get pissed. Most people are charming, even the duds, and there are enormous compensations like Judith Crist for lunch at Pavilion, erudite, warm, with more knowledge of the cinema than many a London equivalent.

But there are the others too: the lady in charge of me, Rona, was delightful and did her best to smooth things over. Which you need if you have to do the *Today* Show from a shop window at seven in the morning! Or even the Johnny Carson show when you get stuck between commercials for Lucky Strike cigarettes and are left to hold a half grown chimpanzee someone brought on to the programme. Not to mention Zsa Zsa Gabor in chiffon, and diamonds to blind you. Difficult to try and plug your *own* product with that competition. Every time I opened my mouth, Carson waved another carton of cigarettes at the camera, or the Chimp rammed its fist into my mouth. We survived. I did my best for MGM even if it didn't show. One gentleman was very sad. Rona asked me to see him, he was not a bit important she added, but kind, and had just gotten divorced. Could I squeeze him in, it'ud make him so thrilled, and he was free-lancing and might sell something if I'd help. I said OK, he could come down to 2nd Avenue during the lunch break while I was doing a fashion session (don't laugh!) for *Vogue*. He arrived at the grubby little studio, smelling of 'pot' and cat's piss (the studio, not the man), four floors above that noisy street. He was shy, tall, pleasant looking, but clearly depressed. Rona flashed a warm smile and left us. He had a small homburg hat with a cord round it, a shiny blue raincoat called, I think, London Fog, too short . . . enormous feet in those huge American shoes, and his trousers were at half mast. Taking off his hat he asked if he could remove his 'rubbers'. I said yes, wondering what they were. Well *we* call them galoshes. How was I to know? Setting them neatly by his chair he drew out his pad and pencil and stared at me for a long time through rimless glasses.

'You look happy,' he said as if I had stolen his watch.

'I am.'

He looked round the grubby little studio, the camera, lights, my suits hanging on a rack. 'You like New York?'

'Yes, very much.'

He shrugged miserably and said he hated it himself. I didn't really see that it concerned me one way or another, I was there to sell MGM's products, but he was not in the least bit interested, that was clear, he had his own problems.

'I just got divorced.'

'I know, Rona told me.'

'She did? She's still waiting for hers ...'

'I'm sorry. About your divorce; unless you are pleased?'

'How could I be?' his eyes glazed with the effrontery of my remark.

'Well ... I don't know ...'

'I'm destroyed. This town did that. This town did it.'

'How? How could the town do it?'

'My wife was a wonderful person, sweet, so nice, gentle. I loved my wife I want you to know.'

'I'm glad.'

'You didn't *know* her. She was one in a million ...' The whole thing was getting both boring and embarrassing, but he wasn't to be stayed; on he went, his eyes filling with tears, the pad and pencil unused in his lap. I was told that they had had a beautiful marriage for four years, it was a dream come true and they were both ecstatically happy, had a superior apartment, never had rows, that she was an architect and really going places. I didn't want the story, but I was stuck there with my ham sandwich from the Plaza and a couple of cans of that ghastly American beer which tastes of cold shaving-water, so I just ate my lunch and let him drone on.

'But what happened, Jud?' He had said his name was Judson but to call him Jud because all his friends did. I had, obviously, and unwittingly, been included as such. American hospitality. The moment that I asked him the question, there was a fearful roaring noise from Second Avenue. I went to the windows to close them with Jud hard behind me. Below, four or five gigantic motorbikes, riders and passengers crouched low, roared up the street weaving and racketing through the scattering traffic. Jud practically screamed. '*That's* what happened! Right there ... that's what happened in this lousy town. Those *shits* happened to my wife!'

It appeared, after we had resumed our places in the studio, that his wife had become involved, without his knowledge, with the Hell's Angels or at any rate the Bike Set. One day she blossomed forth in black leather, chains and cap and had bought a motorcycle which she drove to her work in Brooklyn. Jud was undone. When he discovered this, they had appalling rows and fights, tears and sobs and all the rest but she would not give up her new found hobby, love, or hang-up, as he called it. When I suggested, tactfully of course, that since he loved her so much he might have tried to help her, and himself, by meeting her half way he looked shocked. But admitted that he had tried at first; had bought himself a Bomber Jacket and gloves and boots and went as passenger on her bike at week-ends: but it didn't last. He hated the 'gang' as he called it, and, I gathered, was scared witless by the machines, the speeds, and the drinking. Eventually she left him for someone called Rocky. His divorce had come through a few days ago. He was destroyed.

'You know, it's hard to realise. She was so happy with me. We were learning to cook things, eggs, chili, pizza, Boeuf Strogonoff that kind of stuff ... and she was interested in my work, my writing ... now; well ... she's into boots and leather and that bike and those people. They'll destroy her.'

His time, thank God, was up, the studio crew were coming back from lunch. I got up and handed him his rubbers which he pulled on thanking me all the while. He said he was sorry to have loused up the interview, but I understood, didn't I? And he'd go through the Library Stock and get the background stuff and, well, he had, after all, met me, and I'd been so sympathetic ... and thank you. I saw him out to the little elevator. At the door he turned, the tiny hat in his hand, his huge feet holding the doors open, 'You've been so kind. Reely kind to let me get that off, I feel better, I really do.'

I said how glad I was, and smiled encouragingly. As I turned away he caught my arm.

'Mr Bogarrrde,' he said in a sad voice, 'would it surprise you very much if I told you that my wife ... was a man?'

A funny town.

And *that* is part of my Public Life. So you must see, as I know that you do really, that our worlds are worlds apart. You must not worry about the one you read about in the papers: the one which is real, is the one you read about in the letters. I am the one you know. Me. It is Me who comes off these pages, I who so laboriously type with no spelling and little grammar and no punctuation whatsoever. It is I who write to you. The other person is not all that different, is fundamentally the same, even though you cannot see it, because that person is seen by differing eyes. But I really am almost the same even in New York. It's just that I have to present a different surface. One you don't seem to care for. Too glossy, too arrogant, too whatever it is which distresses you. How could I have possibly been in this profession, give or take the war years, for thirty-five of them and remained the person you know me to be? Nothing of the person you know is taken away from *you* by interviews in the Press, or on Television, or on the Stage or in my work for the screen. It is my work. All of it. Like yours at the University. I have my job and I do it ... doing it sometimes means that I have to be different people to different people at different times. Do you follow me? But I couldn't be all these other people if I were not the one solid person at the base. Do you see what I mean? I know who I am, I shall not lose myself. Or my standards, or my faith or my integrity. I stay me. As I am. As I was brought up to be. I am inflexible on that point ... but flexible when my work demands it to be so. I know that you have been worried, frightened, and in pain. But don't, I beg of you, let me add to your distresses; that is the last thing on God's earth I would wish to do. But my work is my work; and I must play it the way I see it; it is not always easy, not always pleasant, never, the Press part, fun. But it has to be done and I do it to the best of my ability. Please try and laugh with me sometimes, I know that you can't at this moment ... but when you are stronger? For I only want to bring you pleasure, even though I must irritate you from time to time, but that is, surely, quite normal? A correspondence course such as this doesn't include the nuance of voice, I know ... or the smile in the voice ... but next time you mis-read something I have written, or have said in the Press or am 'quoted' as saying ... take this letter out and re-read it. For comfort. And for assurance ...

29

The House

March 12th '68

The idea of you wandering about the corridors of the Memorial Unit in your nightwear like Grace Pool rather worried me. However, the fact that you could wander at all was, I suppose, reassuring even though you did get severely reprimanded. So there we are. All over. And you minus, as you say, 'some rather attractive sparking plugs and no belly button!' Christ! Have they taken that away too? Are you sort of pleated together down the middle. A kind of Banjo? No, I know that you can't laugh, nor must you, nor must I attempt to make you. Plunk! go the stitches. But at least you have got through it all, the weight of misery and apprehension is gone, thank God, and you seem to be almost back to normal ... at least your handwriting is steadier than of late ... I am glad that the starlings helped and that they at least got there ... there is so little one can do at times like that. Operations are something one has to face alone, like birth and death I suppose. Comfort and care and all the other things can only be offered and accepted, but they do so little to mitigate the great grey swamp of fear and doubt that swaddles one all the time. I felt so futile sending you daily views of Dinard, Tunbridge Wells, or Flatford Mill ... you must have hundreds surely? Perhaps you could play Patience with them? Or, better still, get the Nurse to cut them all up into little pieces, shake them up in a bag, and then play Puzzles with them. Or better still chuck them all into the air and read a good book. Or a bad one. I sent you, incidentally, Massie's *Nicholas and Alexandra* and realised, too late, that it is a dreadfully heavy tome and will weigh heavy on the Banjo ... but it is good hospital reading if a bit depressing. Well. One knows the end doesn't one? That cellar in Ekaterinburg ... all the time I was reading it I kept wanting to shake Alexandra and say, 'No! Don't! Don't do it ...' as if I could have changed her destiny. Poor, silly cow. I wonder if Anastasia really is that lady in the Black Forest? I bet she is ... who could possibly say she was absolutely not? There is too much loot, if one is to believe the stories, lying about in a British Bank, and too many interested parties, to allow her to be accepted.

By now, I hope very much, you are out of the Memorial Thing ... it did rather sound like a crematorium ... and back in the loving care of Anna. How lucky you are to have her to care for you and the house while you have been away ... I love her morning signal with your break-fast tray. A single rose to announce that there is a letter from me. None if there is not! She must order them in sheaves! What does she use to signal merely a starling? A blade of grass? Of course 'she knows what's going on' for all her Polish good manners. Why else did she bring 'stacks of airmail envelopes and sheets and sheets of letter paper and pencils PLUS stamps for England'. What did she expect you to do with them even though you do have 'a lot of other friends there'? She knows all right. She posts the things doesn't she? Knows the address and the name I bet by heart ... don't be so soppy. She ain't daft, Polish or not.

Oh dear me. I've asked questions again. Not for answer-ing. Rhetorical only. Do you realise that we have been writing to each other for over a year now? It has gone so quickly ... I hate the scoundrel Time; he plays filthy tricks on one when you get to my age ...

30

The House

March 21st '68

A tremendous gale rocks the house, hail lashes at the windows, the timbers creak, and I get more and more grumpy, irritated and disagreeable by the hour. I detest high winds: I could never play Heathcliff. Or even poor tiresome Branwell. Even your super-duper Maceys-End-Of-Winter Letter hardly managed to cheer me. Well it did. Of course it did. I'm just grottling on: super that strength returns, but you must be patient.

Not much to report this week really. Up to town on Tuesday for a Memorial Service (oh dear! another ...). This time for Anthony Asquith in St Margaret's beside the Abbey. Very formal, un-theatrical, Family and so on. Actually I have a feeling that the Family wanted to keep the Actors out of the show, but it got about and we were all there anyhow. He was very much loved and respected by us all, and will be most wretchedly missed. Good taste is not easy to find in our profession: Asquith has taken a great deal of it away with him I fear. Lady Violet was in the front row, sort of matriarch. Lost, lonely and visibly deeply distressed. Young children, nieces and nephews I suppose: half, or maybe all, the Liberal Party present. Joe Grimond in front of me, Asquith's aged and devoted Housekeeper beside me, Rex Harrison on the other side, all in black and very elegant. Redgrave read the Lesson, we sang some hymns, a good choir with sweet soaring voices ... sun gleaming through the coloured windows

... muffled rumble of passing traffic ... sparrows chirping. When it was all done and we had sat down in a decorous rustle of coats and hymn books, a slight figure suddenly arrived from behind the altar. Crumpled blue suit, a violin in his hand. He stood shyly in a patch of filtered sunlight and played Bach's Chaconne (in D Minor). One of Asquith's favourite pieces. When he came to the house on Sundays sometimes he used always to bring two or three of his favourite records and play them, he never quite trusted my rather catholic collection, and this was one of them and very familiar. Yehudi Menuhin was saluting his lost friend. We sat there spellbound. We had just heard Olivier read that bit from Corinthians about Charity and that had nearly un-manned us all ... but this compounded the lumps in our throats. Fortunately Rex leaned towards me and touched my arm gently. 'Never could abide a fiddler!' he whispered, and sort of broke the grief, beautifully. I was very grateful.

31

The House

Easter Monday
April 15th '68

A golden Easter for a change this year, but clouded
miserably by the news of Martin Luther King. It was hard
to take in at first, another assassination. One is utterly
bewildered. Among the house-guests down for the
holiday was a lady from North Carolina now married, to
an English man, and happily settled in Hurlingham, who
was bitterly distressed. 'Why, in God's name,' she cried,
'do we just shoot everyone we don't agree with in our
country?' A sad cry, and one which was difficult to answer.
But, apart from that, it was a pleasant time although
extremely hard work and bloody expensive. Fifteen for
Sunday. Lunch, tea and dinner. Antonia and Eduardo
spinning like tops, drink flowing like a river, splendid
food and so on but is it all worth it? I mean I LOVE
them all ... but I do actually like being alone better. I use
myself up somehow, and there is a big gap before I am
able to replenish myself. And the expense is appalling ...
I'll have to start cutting it down, entertaining I mean.
This happens every single week-end in life, never less than
eight to ten, and all day ... madness.

Incidentally, thinking about money, I have turned
down the script from Visconti after a bit of thought ...
it's too diffuse, crammed with stuff, and the part is really
not a bit good. So I have agreed to do Renoir's *Memoirs
of Captain Jacques* which is, I think, absolutely beautiful,
if very slight. But in his hands one 'feels' it will work

107

marvellously. He wants Jeanne Moreau for the girl ...
I'm a bit doubtful that she may look, or be even, a bit too
old for it. However, she is a staggering actress and it is
good for the finance to have her name. We'll see. I know
that in my present financial situation, and having no offers
of work from England, I ought not to be so cavalier about
the film from Visconti ... but I am terrified of working
abroad anyway, and dare not risk a failure first time off
... and the Renoir thing is good for me, and the two can
not be fitted in together this year.

By the way, the film I told you about with Alain Resnais
has reared its splendid head again. MGM, of all people,
have said they MIGHT finance it if he will make some
cuts in the length. At the moment it runs, as we say,
almost four hours or more ... and will cost a fortune, so
their demands are not, on the face of things, unreasonable
... He wants to have Vanessa Redgrave with me, which
delights me ... so all in all the summer may be less gloomy
than I had anticipated, in spite of the fact that all these
subjects are for Abroad. As I warned you.

I looked at the daffodils down in the nut walk and
under the chestnut trees this morning and thought that I
might extend them even further this autumn. Plant a few
more sackfuls in September ... for next spring? But will
I see them next spring I wonder? I feel terribly restless
and unable to settle: like a dog before a storm. I don't
know what to do ... I know what I SHOULD do, but
it seems so terribly drastic a move. After all, I have lived
here for nearly fifty years ... I mean in England ... it
would be a hellish wrench to leave it ...

I feel wretched suddenly! Talking to you like this has
got me into a state. I think I'll finish this off and clear off
into the garden, there is a lot to do there, and sticking my
hands in earth seems to heal me quicker than any other
activity. I'll only drone on like this if I continue, and there
is sweet bugger all that you can do to help me ... even
though I know that you would if you could. Incidentally,

while I am at that point, I am delighted beyond any measure that you are killing yourself with the kindness of good friends and neighbours, not to mention all your nosy students! But don't go and do yourself a mischief, it's a bit soon for larking about ... ration your pleasures you idiot, otherwise Anna will be sending me black-edge letters ...

32

The House

April 25th '68

A blazing day. Heat shimmers. The carts are out in the meadows spraying the fertiliser muck about, which rather spoils the effect ... but lambs bleat on the high ridges, every bird you ever heard of is singing and falling about on the edge of the pond bathing. The stocks are this high, cornflowers in bud, asparagus brandishing, albeit timidly, the first pink shoots ... and the early peas have cracked through the dry soil and my February onions (sucks to you for sarcasm) and shallots march in green pride in neat serried rows down the slope to the stream. I hate to leave it at this time ... but I'm off to Rome on Saturday. Taking the car. Be away ten days, and will tell you why when I get there. I'll go by way of Genoa and stay off for a few days in the south of France at St Paul de Vence. To have a look about me ... see what there is to see. You know? Yes you do, even if you won't admit it. But trust me.

A telephone call from Elizabeth yesterday to say that Lally's husband, Alf, is critically ill with, of course, cancer. They simply adore each other and haven't been married very long, both setting off rather late in life on that adventure. It seems so bloody unfair. Naturally I offered help. Elizabeth said that Lally had considered it thoughtfully and said she'd let her know. She has intense pride. Anyhow this morning she telephoned to say that she had thought of something she'd really like and needed badly. 'A basket for my bike, dear, so that I can put the groceries in it instead of having to walk with them in a bag.' A basket for her bike. Well, she has one now ... What a long time ago it seems since we were what she called 'her' children, Elizabeth and I. The years of innocence have sped. We'd never heard of cancer, a Race was something you ran and lost or won, Communists were people who lived somewhere near China and we didn't know where that was anyway, a Golliwog was something in a striped weskit you took to bed to comfort yourself. But we knew about Ouzles and Thrushes and the difference between them, about cuckoo-spit and cowslips, about roach and perch, about emptying the 'night soil' and brewing ginger beer ... oh shit! If only we could have it all back.

33

The House

May 18th '68

Difficult to believe, driving through the sunlit fields of France yesterday, that something very like a revolution is rumbling about in Paris. The city itself was, on the surface, calm. People in the streets, but walking quietly and very slowly. No one ran. Traffic subdued. Sunlight, sounds of feet on the pavements, air of undercurrent tension; a waiting. Not pleasant. Near the Sorbonne it is all a bit more visible. Cobble stones ripped up, trees ripped down, branches everywhere, burned out cars, smashed windows, glass in glittering piles, the smell of burning rubber, oil ... charred banners, café chairs and tables jumbled up with iron grills in hasty barricades. Not the first time the city has seen this, and clearly not the last I fear ...

Resnais was very sad and ashen faced. Has decided not to go ahead with the film project we had in mind because M G M have asked for too many 'cuts' and conditions and anyway he feels the guts have dropped out of his ambition. I really think it is something more than that, and that the events of the last few days have distressed him greatly, as indeed they have all Frenchmen of all kinds and persuasions. Things are *very* tense. I am completely on the side of the students, their demands are fair and realistic. The curricula (is that how you spell it?) is archaic and impossible. But it is the Communists who have joined in for their own cause who may just cause the whole thing to erupt into far worse bloodshed than we have yet seen:

they will reap the benefit of the storm ... not the unhappy students who actually started it off. That's typical infiltration. Exploiting a minor wound, infecting it, and setting up a form of gangrene. One prays that good sense will prevail in this fine country; the next few days will tell. Managed to get the last boat out of Boulogne in the afternoon just before the general strike closed the whole country. No planes, boats, telephones, post, all shops and banks are closed. One waits. And of course the Renoir film has been postponed. You can't really think of making a movie when the country is sliding towards the fire. The tinder is dry as brushwood. It'll only take one match.

Rome was quite fun. Very hot, very full of tourists, but still as achingly beautiful as ever. I can now confess, which I was far too ashamed to do before as you gather, that I went there to do ... oh Lord! a Commercial for American Television. There: it is out. My shame is complete. Shan't tell you for what or for whom, lest you get one of your students to give you a full report ... and since I don't utter a word, and do not extol the virtues of the product I am, reluctantly, selling, I shall be hard to trace if I keep my trap shut! It was not as humiliating as I feared. I just ran up and down the Spanish Steps for a morning and got paid a delectable amount of money, which is why I had to do it ... but never again.

However, being there did give me the chance of seeing some of my friends again, and, more importantly, of receiving yet another version of the script from Visconti: this time much better ... and since he is very anxious for me to do it, and as I discovered him to be *quite* electrifying and exciting at our first meeting, I said yes right away. He is an amazing man. I was completely captivated. However the film itself turns out, it won't be anything like the unhappy experience in Budapest. This is no amateur at work. This gentleman is a professional from the top of his steely eyed head to the toes of his elegant shoes. So I'm in. We start in July. So I won't have very much time left here. The onions and the shallots will have to manage without me ... for quite a time as it happens, for I have also agreed to play 'Pursewarden' in your favourite books! The *Alexandria Quartet* of Durrell ... that was a surprise in the Roman-Package ... naturally it is a very abbreviated version of the books. But the one I have read, script I mean, is not bad at all. At least it has some of Durrell's 'feel' about it, and I think I can make a reasonable Pursewarden, don't you? Fortunately it is all being made in Tunis (for Alexandria) and Paris (for the Studio) as long as things have sorted themselves out by November anyway. So I'll be in suitcases for quite a while now. A prospect which doesn't really distress me ... the restlessness which has beset me for so long is somehow assuaged. I want to work. And the offers from Foreign Parts are very flattering. Naturally I'd far rather work for England ... but at what? So ...

I am sad that you are still in pain. But as you say, that is to be expected for a bit longer. You didn't have a Face-Lift my dear: you had a whole Belly-lift. Of course it'll take time, but at least you have the two Stracheys to keep you company. Glad they arrived, glad you like them. The first book is a bit dull, second far better, and of course, you are right, the first one should be read AFTER-WARDS, as you divined. Poor Carrington! A sad, besotted lady. Quite a lot of them about today. It's a special breed. I do think her painting was rather good though, don't you? It's rather dismissed today. I remember V. Woolf when I was a child when we lived at Lullington. She was 'over the big Down' at Rodmell in the Ouse valley. Used to see her marching about the water-meadows quite often. Hair wispy and caught into a loose sort of knot, a big stick or sometimes a brightly coloured umbrella furled. A golf umbrella I imagine, a droopy cardigan. She sometimes wore a big floppy straw hat and we all thought she was a witch. Or could put spells on you ... there was a strange décontracté air about her which made us all uneasy. When I say all, I mean the village boys, with whom I was not strictly speaking allowed to play on account of they'd teach me 'nasty habits' according to Lally. She never spoke to us, but sometimes sang to herself, a sure sign that she was 'barmy' as we said . . . and picked little bunches of wild flowers. I was on leave in 1941 when she drowned herself, by which time of course I knew who she was, and was strangely affected when I read in the paper that she had filled the pockets of her droopy cardigan with stones in order to weigh her down in the river in which we had fished, so long ago, for a monster Pike . . . such a pathetic desperation; two pocket-fuls of stones.

I'm reading now, and will send you later, Cynthia Asquith's Diaries, 1915–18 which I am loving and think that you will too. She was a cousin of Anthony Asquith, whose mum was the fearsome Margot Asquith, a brilliant, witty, ugly and often cruel-tongued lady, quite unlike her son who was an angel of good manners and kindness. I once saw him trip over a cable in the studios and turn swiftly, hands to his mouth with distress, to apologise to it! 'Oh I A M so sorry . . . so sorry! I do beg your pardon!' he exclaimed. He did, however, share his mother's extremely pronounced nose which is why he was always known as 'Puffin' . . . and he was, indeed, not at all unlike one of those enchanting, strutting, little birds.

Broke off there for a moment. Now it's the 20th. This is all a bit bitty . . . went to London to Harold Pinter's house-warming party. A splendid house in Hanover Terrace . . . I imagine it to be beautiful inside, but it was hard to tell for the crush of people, all yelling and shouting and laughing and jammed into every nook and cranny, treading olives into the new carpets and spilling cham-pagne all over the Regency veneers. Everyone seemed to be there from John Gielgud to the Beatles. Harold beaming in his usual placid way. He is a most enchanting man, a really 'good inside' person, if you know what that means, and I am sure that he was as bemused as I was to realise that not very long ago he was a struggling actor in a Northern Rep. It was a big jump. As I was struggling in a long, crushed, queue to get some food from the huge tables with a pleasant young man who turned out to be Paul McCartney, a rather 'high' lady, neither of us knew, pushed between us and said in a rather loud voice, 'And all this bounty, my dears, is what comes from being enigmatic ...' and wandered away ... Anyway; I'm tired and still a bit hung over. I hate parties, but love Harold and his wife Vivien, so got trapped.

I think I'd better pack this in and find a glass of Fernet Branca. But you can get 'hooked' on that too ...

34

The House

May 31st '68

It appears that De Gaulle has suddenly reasserted his authority and my beloved France seems headed either for La Gloire or Civil War. I can see no alternative. An extraordinary situation ... one prays not a tragic one. If only, if only, *we* had someone as powerful, as brave, as passionate about his country, someone with guts and force. What a change there would be in England. I suppose Philip ... our not-over-loved Consort, could do something. I wish to Heaven we really had a proper, old-fashioned, Off-With-His-Head-Monarchy again. Which reminds me, with utter dread, that I have to go and have lunch with H M on the 6th. One D-day (in 1944) was bad enough. I simply dread it. I'm no good at this kind of function. I tried to get out of it but to no avail. Was asked to go in April, by her equerry, Patrick Plunket, with whom I was in the war. Managed to wriggle clear by pleading that I simply had to work. I wasn't but managed to make it stick. He fixed me for June. He was very shocked when I tried it again, and when I told him to get me excused, he explained patiently, but with a certain amount of grittiness, that I was 'commanded' to appear for lunch, and that the Queen was disappointed about the last time. I bet. Don't suppose she knows who I am even. This set of lunches is all a part of Philip's 'democratisation' (if that is a word!) of the Royals. They get to meet The People at the lunch table.

Oh hell. I suppose it'll be a Famous Footballer, a Jockey and a District Nurse and tinned pears and custard. And I don't know anything about corgis much, and absolutely nothing at all about horses. It'll be a sparkling lunch. We could, I suppose, or I could, always have a chat about the housekeepers she has known! I had a couple of ex-Royals in my time. Mrs K. who was a true Mary Poppins, tall, thin, neat in black with a straw hat, petersham ribbon, big jet hat-pin, lace up shoes. She'd been housekeeper to Queen Mary at Marlborough House for many years, and got badly stabbed in a burglary they had there after the old Queen died. It was all a bit of a headline-story in the Press and she delighted in telling it all, plus the details about blood and blade. She was a determined creature; demanded, and got I may add, a maid to herself to bring her her morning tea and massage her 'old legs' ... which made Hilda, her maid (who had been my Parlour Maid) furious. She ran up vast bills at Fortnum's and Harrods, carted some of the slightly-chipped Meissen birds off to Goodes for restoration (which cost a fortune!) and finally broke my back when she ordered 100 pairs of white cotton pillow cases for the staff beds. Since the staff, at that time, consisted solely of herself, Hilda and Fred my parlour man, and a louche youth who helped about the house doing fires and splitting logs and in any case didn't sleep in, I really felt she had gone too far ... but she was a good cook, and apart from boring the Staff Room witless with her memories and souvenirs of the Royals, she was a kind and nice woman ... far nicer than Mrs R. who was a fat, cross Scots woman who looked like a cottage loaf and had worked for years for the Kents. She regaled us all with the full details of life at Coppins and took an instant, and unrelenting, dislike to me. So that I never dared go into the kitchen, or question her menus ... and she ruled the Staff Room with a rod of iron and had Hilda in floods of tears nearly every day ... so she went. And a nice lady called Mrs G. arrived as a temporary straight from

10 Downing Street where she had, very briefly, worked for Mr Wilson ... who sacked her because her cooking was 'not plain enough'. Unlike Mrs R. she was not a bit gossipy ... which was good and disappointing at the same time ... but she did confirm H P sauce on the table at No. 10, and boiled potatoes and kippers and so on ... and thought wistfully, and with a longing I share, how nice it would be to have a Gentleman back there, like Sir Alec Douglas-Home ... whom she adored. But it was Mrs K. who has finally filled me with gloom for the dreaded 6th luncheon. She served tinned pears and custard constantly at Marlborough House ... why should it be any different just down the road at Buckingham Palace?

35

On Wednesday morning the butcher told me about the attempted assassination of Bobby K. I hadn't heard the radio that night ... that rather slammed the lid on the day. Sent a cable off to poor Jean [Kennedy Smith] who has been writing so cheerfully about the Campaign and with such high hopes. What does one say the second time around? I just said 'There are no words' ... and there aren't. It is quite clear that someone disapproves of the Californian triumph. Why, as someone said when Luther King was shot, do they have to shoot everyone they don't agree with in your adopted country?

Yesterday, driving up to my tinned-pears and custard lunch with Her Majesty, I had the radio on all the time for news flashes, and just as we had got through Edenbridge, at ten a.m., they cut in and said that he was dead. For a moment one bowed one's head ... an instinctive gesture ... the music was very soft and solemn, I think it was Sibelius. Can't remember really. (Waiting, as we all had been, for a final announcement, the BBC had cut the normal programmes.) Looking up the sky seemed not quite so blue; the buttercups along the hedgerows not quite so golden. I saw a woman with a small boy and a dog running and laughing along a path, and wanted to yell at them, 'Shut up! Stop it! He's dead ...' Of course, they didn't know.

When we turned into Park Lane about an hour later

Labo, back from the vet, Villa Fratelli, May 5th, 1969

Xan and Daphne Fielding, Villa Fratelli, 1969

The Villa Fratelli from the east, 1969

My parents at Villa Fratelli, June 1969

Visconti's garden at Castelgandolfo, looking over the volcanic lake

Near Frenchman's Cove, Port Antonio, Jamaica, January 30th, 1968

Lunch on the beach at Frenchman's Cove, 1968

(*Above*) As 'Pursewarden' in
Justine with Kathleen Tynan
and Patrick Lichfield outside
the *souk*, Tunis, 1968

(*Right*) With Anouk Aimée
(playing 'Justine'),
Hollywood, 1968 (Justine,
copyright © Twentieth Century
Fox Film Corporation. All
rights reserved

Film-clip from *Upon This Rock* at the tomb of Bonnie Prince Charlie in St Peter's, Rome, 22nd December, 1969 (*NBC*)

With Visconti in the steel-works (*The Damned*), January 30th, 1969 (*Mario Tursi*)

With Jack Clayton in Croydon market, on location for *Our Mother's House*, December 1966 (*MGM*)

With Harold Pinter in *Accident*, 1966 (*London Independent Producers*)

March 2., the first day of spring, intermittent sun fanned by a sharp
wind, and the poor little nubbins of hyacinth and crocus looking a bit
anxious and green-nosed

This is merely blanched blue-jay...for non-answering. I know that you
say "never explain!" But without my trying to, you'll think me more
ridiculous than ever and completely unable to understand the néant
in which I've been floating....a silly "unanchored" tadpole.

A phrase in your last LETTER set me thinking about marriage. From all
I see and read and hear....it's for the birds.

For all our ridiculous "carnet de famille, ▓ and I never were nor felt
married. It was a coup de foudre, which is apparently extremely rare...
that Platonic half-atom encountering its other half in the whirling
universe...a felicitous and perfect passionate fusion. Natural, inevitable.
If you've experienced it, you know. If not, impossible to convey. It
flowered in an ideal ambience.....leisure, ability to gratify every fleeting
whim, isolation from people, a walled garden with gloire de Dijon roses
and espaliered fruit trees, and our devoted housekeeper, Sidonie,...
"ah, Madame, l'amour...que c'est du bon dieu, ça."

But nothing lasts forever, and you already know how grim were the seven
years of severance. One found a foothold. Scars formed. One was
thankful to be a vacuum, and rejected all human relationships lest one
should ever feel again.

All the rest, you also know, patient darling....how reluctantly one
was seduced, after all the frozen years, into an utterly fresh and
joyous emotional involvement...the glacier, thawing under untold
hearts kindness, pouring, unasked, probably unwanted, but somehow understood, towards the owner of ▓....

On February 24th, ▓▓▓▓▓ died. I hadn't seen him in twenty years,
I was always prepared for this eventuality.....'knowing"there could be
no further grief.—Oddly enough, I felt as though I had been kicked....
and tried to laugh at myself, to reason....but mind over matter is a
nice theory. The banjo rebelled, the muscles ached. Probably a virus..
so I went to the doctors. Blood pressure soaring, nothing else wrong.
"It looks like severe emotional shock with muscular tensions. Have you
had a shock recently?" So I told him, adding "but that was weeks ago".
He laughed" "Never can tell what the subconscious will do." Perhaps.

Anyhow, that's what's knocked the tadpole adrift. You are still so
close to your own loss that you probably know how memories come flooding...
the happier they are, the worse the pain. The guilt that one is still
living...and for me, the bleakness of not being needed by anyone. It's
hard to learn that aloneness is not an absolute term, but a relative one.

So, continue to laugh at me, as I try to ridicule myself. You must
know how difficult it is to face finality with a sense of humour! My
immediate instinct was to write to you...but I pictured you as happy
with your garden, and didn't want to bother you. I wish I had your
outlet of tears! Here, there wasn't a soul to talk to, and I suppose
that au fond, man is a "social animal" and needs a certain amount of
communication...else why was he endowed with speech.

These are all stupid words,.....all I know is that I love et al....and
that he'll manage to understand "the underside of the leaf".

Health and happiness to you, darling! *and Sue!*

they were lowering all the flags to half mast. At the Dorchester, Grosvenor House ... on the Banks. All over the city they started to slide down the poles as if on a sudden command. People stood about in small huddles watching. Some openly weeping. Not all of them Americans I might just add. The shame and the despair; the sheer utter hopelessness. A world without standards. How terribly that family has been struck ... and so often. Yesterday in London one wanted to comfort every bewildered, blue rinsed Matron from Oregon or Maine, every shattered tartan-trousered man ... they stood like abandoned dolls. Stranded at corners, by traffic lights, outside shops ... People wanted to share their grief, and did. It was very moving to see a perfectly ordinary London postman, a sack of mail at his feet, one arm round the bowed back of a weeping lady with camera and guidebook. The family, quite irrespective of politics, had captured Europe's imagination ... it really did feel as if, at last, America was founding a dynasty for itself. And the grief was for us all ... we have all lost out by the bullets in that bloody kitchen in Los Angeles. Somebody somewhere must be very happy ... At the Embassy in Grosvenor Square an immense queue had already formed in the hour the news had broken, apparently to sign the book.

But the day went on its course. Days, thankfully, do. I set off to my dreaded lunch ... half hoping, well hoping entirely really!, that it might be cancelled because of the news ... but alas! her standard was streaming high in the summer breeze. I will admit, although I feel a bit guilty, that sweeping through the great gilded gates in my own car, in my best dark suit, was quite fun. And the tremendous Present Arms I got from the guard, and the smashing wink I received from the guard commander under his busby sent the Japanese Tourists absolutely frantic with their Nikons and Pentaxes ... flashes popped like flak bursts! Kennedy quite forgotten. Although perhaps the Japanese don't share our grief to the same extent?

However. As we made a wide curve across the gravel to the red carpet and the distant figure of Patrick waiting for me, Louis, my driver, immaculate in his new cap for the occasion and new cockade, turned in his seat, and with a deferential cough, signalling a question, he asked what he should call me AFTER lunch. I told him that it really was only that, and no kneeling and sword tapping ... and he sighed wistfully.

Patrick was rather glum faced, I thought ... 'So glad you got here in *time* ... don't look so disagreeable, you're not going to the block you know.'

Miles of corridors and carpets ... like an annex of St Peter's. And then the private apartments, wide windows open on to sunlit lawns, great trees, the shimmer of the distant lake. The room comfortable, small; turkey carpet, fat chairs, great jardiniers stuffed with tall clumps of Nicotina (white) much as Vivien used to have at Notley in the summer. Maybe she pinched the Idea from here? A sort of country-house atmosphere, with a tray of glasses and crystal decanters ... some other drinks in bottles. Very informal. Patrick told me that I was to call her Majesty at the introduction and then forget it ... Ma'am from then on; an informal, private affair. There were only three other guests ... and not one footballer! Julian Bream the guitarist (classical not electric), Max Aitken of the Beaverbrook Press ... looking neat and simian ... I was momentarily astonished to see him present after all the unpleasant attacks he makes on the family in his papers; however ... and a nice gentleman who was once my commanding officer, years ago in Catterick, and was now something very high up in the War Graves Commission ... we had not met since 1941. ... so that was quite relaxing over Tio Pepe. I must confess that I had a swift amused thought that I had come quite a way since those days as an inept Signals corporal. And a long way too from bangers and beans in the pub opposite my first Rep. theatre.

Then she came in ... among a scattering of the familiar corgis, with Princess Alexandra just, apparently, back from Germany where, poor girl, she had been reviewing some Regiment ... they were laughing very much about something, and Alexandra straightened her hat and put her gloves in her pocket.

The first thing that strikes one is her astonishing prettiness: not at all apparent from a million press photographs or newsreels. And she is quite tiny ... neat and elegant. A simple, sleeveless black dress and a whacking great diamond clip on her left shoulder. Pearls and the handbag. But she didn't for one second look like the cook she so often does in those floating silk coats and hats like chamber-pots-inverted which she is forced to wear in public. It seemed a terrible pity that they had never seen her as smart, chic, relaxed and jolly as she was that morning. My good fortune I know. For that alone I felt rather smug ... and enjoyed my lunch. A simple affair, eight of us (with the lady in waiting and a pleasant Colonel from Sussex). No vastly important conversation, general chit-chat really as we went from smoked salmon, inevitably, to a lemon soufflé which was pretty well risen but molten glue inside. There was a Hock, a Claret ... and we all used just the one set of eating irons, simple silver knives with George III stamped on them, and wiped on your bread between courses. Sensible. And I set up three of each at home. Middle Class?

Afterwards back to the sitting room again for coffee ... the sun striping the faded turkey carpet ... sparkling on polished wood and the brass fender: in the empty fireplace, a neat pleated paper fan.

Naturally we talked about the Kennedy business, and agreed how dreadfully difficult it was to find words for yet another telegram of condolence. The Official one was all right, but the personal one far harder. I said what I'd sent and she thought it correct. And then about Paris and the events of last month, and how good it was that there were no longer any cobble-stones left in the streets of London ... it was all very relaxed and pleasant; she stood there in the windows, the sun on her face, her eyes a startling cornflower blue (something else that doesn't show on photographs), one foot comfortably out of a shoe, the corgis lying about on the terrace with their shot-rabbit-legs, and I suddenly fully realised, looking across to the lake and the lawns and the summer trees beyond, shimmering in the afternoon, just what Shakespeare had meant by 'this sceptred isle'. At three she looked at her watch, said that she was going to the Thynne wedding at St James's, and was I? And I said not, I'd been invited but had declined because I was so dreading lunching with her and one event in the day was enough, and she laughed and said I really ought to come because she had heard that The Rolling Stones might be there, and she rather longed to see them ... by this time, of course, I was so enchanted and under her very potent spell that I nearly changed my mind. But really couldn't face it and drove out into the town of half-mast flags very contented with my lot and a confirmed Royalist. If she and Philip really had power of any kind and really could rule, I'm damned sure I'd stay; in fact I know I would ...

I have my marching orders for Rome and Visconti on July 15th. Which could mean that I may well not see the house again, unless I am very lucky, until probably January ... But I won't dwell on that just yet ... there is a lurking sadness. I'll have it out into the light of day shortly ... must face things ... but not, perhaps, for the moment. There is still a little time left before the break ...

36

The House

June 11th '68

I am so glad that you are liking *Nancy and Emerald* ... a boring, and almost terrible, couple I suppose in a tragic way. I confess that I got to simply detest Emerald towards the end of the book, which is quite an achievement because Daph [Fielding] refused to be 'cruel', as she put it, about her and steadfastly tried to whitewash them both during all the weeks of long research she had to make. I rather ticked her off for that, as a matter of fact, but she said that she simply couldn't be beastly 'to chums' and that's maybe what will go wrong with the book. I think it doesn't tell you enough ... However, Emerald's great cry of despair and indignation, 'How can they do this to me?', when Edward VIII abdicated, gives you a glimpse of the silly woman, in spite of Daph's care. However it is a slim book, and I only sent it to you for bed-reading. Light on the banjo I hope ... and light on the intellect. Never mind. If, in my letters, I seem, as you say, a bit gregarious it is because that's how I am at the moment ... hopping about getting things done, seeing lots of people, dealing with Staff, gardens and all before pushing off. There are a lot of little knots to tie up.

My lovely Spaniards are on hol. in Valencia, to have a bit of a break before sitting here on their backsides all alone until January. I have a splendid Temporary Gentleman called Kenneth Sheridan Jones who was sent by the Agency to help out. He's as black as your hat, ten foot tall, extremely nice, willing and capable ... comes from Antigua and was, I think, once a Body-builder. At any rate he does exercises all the time he isn't cooking or polishing, and has a great box of iron bars and wheels and things in the Staff Sitting-room. His main extravagance, as far as I can see, is one dozen raw eggs consumed every morning with a quart of milk. To keep his waist at thirty and his chest at, one imagines, three hundred. He is a very impressive sight doing his press-ups on the lawn in nothing but a silver chain and a jock-strap. The baker got quite a shock.

Daph, as a matter of fact, is coming down next week-end; she came over from France for Christopher's (Thynne's) wedding at St James's. The one I didn't go to. It was all a bit of a muck-up ... there is a current rumour about Town that someone laced the cake with LSD ... which, if true, could mean that the Queen took her first 'trip'. What is certain is that poor old Christopher was arrested at the airport setting off on his honeymoon in Majorca ... some pleasant sod tipped them off that he was smuggling drugs ... and they did find something in his camera-case, planted we all feel sure. He's on bail, and on his beach I hope, but comes back to face the Court on July 1st. Bloody luck. We are all quite sure that it was a jolly prank by one of his peculiar chums. The Permissive Age is really very tacky.

Incidentally the lady you think was American and horrible was not Margot Asquith. She was Nancy Astor of Cliveden. Not the same thing at all; but fairly nasty, and American. What a snobby little letter this is. Almost as gossipy as the Channon book you so rightly found repellent. I knew it was a mistake when I sent it off. Next time you'll get a nice simple D. L. Sayers. But come to think of it, she's quite snobby too ...

37

The House

June 20th '68

You really are a bit of a cheat. I should never have sent
you that bloody photograph (all that begging and pleading
... so that you could have it 'by me in the Clinic'), I knew
it was breaking the rules ... and you knew too ... but
such is the force of your personality that I overcame my
reluctance and now, I am informed, I stand 'tucked into
a neat green-leather frame, on the writing table'. Well
thanks. Thanks a load. Exposed to all the world! All your
curious students having a good gander. Anna ... and all
to pleasure you during your wretched l'heure verte. Well.
All I can say is I was MUCH better off, as you first had
me, tucked neatly into the pages of Mr Klee's works.
Anyway: it's you who will look the muggins, not me.
Remember how shocked B.'s cousin in Edinburgh was
when you just casually 'mentioned my name' in a letter?
Respectable women don't know Fillum Stars ... and they
don't write to them, ever. Only nit-wits do that. But you
are a nit-wit.

But of course you have completely won me over by un-
willing me that blasted Modigliani (which was, anyway,
far too small for my liking), and the Picasso Lithograph.
Thanks. You are quite right, a black and white Picasso
would bore me unendurably. And it is very thoughtful of
you to realise that I could be saddled with trillions of
dollars of Duty just exactly at a time when you would not
be around to sort things out. Sometimes your intelligence

and thoughtfulness positively winds me. I have to do quick reassessments of you and that is exhausting.

But why bang on about Wills and things? That isn't the sort of thinking for l'heure verte, surely? L'heure bleue more like. After all, you have walked round the block already ... which is a huge achievement even if it was at snail's pace. At least you were out and about. Isn't that hopeful? No, of course, I'd like to share one of your vertes with you ... but can one do that? I mean share them? I thought one only had them on one's own ... I get hopelessly muddled. Anyway, I'll think of you when I have mine: you sitting by my photograph in my bloody leather frame, sipping your whisky-laced-tea, and doing your Tennessee Williams act.

But you know, you'd get awfully fed up with me ... it wouldn't be quite as gay as you seem to think. Me sitting in the big chair beside you, evening after evening. You'd find me very irritating. My Dom, my moods ... my utter laziness, I'd be a colossal irritant. Think of all the books you wouldn't be able to read if I were there sitting grumbling. I honestly think, when all is said and done, that Letters are the best. Truly. But don't fuss about the misapprehensions, misunderstandings that sometimes occur. They are bound to in a situation like this one. How can I possibly indicate, unless I gave you explicit instructions like 'Laugh here' or 'Nudge, nudge, this is to be read with tongue in cheek', a smile, when I write? Nor can you see the glow of pleasure on my face when I read your letters to me. Perhaps that is the only time I should share your l'heure verte ... when I am reading your mail. On the other hand this letter to you won't bring the customary glow of joy to your cheek ... I'm in a grittsville mood today. I feel sad, bothered too. I have to work again soon, that's really at the back of it ... I don't count the Budapest stint, it was a small role, and, as you remember, I was very little involved with the unhappy thing. But this next job is a bit bigger. I have a poor role, and a demanding Director. I have to work hard. Very hard. And in a foreign land ... I must not fail. And the feeling that the future is so dim is unsettling. I know I'm making the right decision to leave, but naturally it scares me, I'm getting a bit old for sudden changes and adventures. I'll get better ... and, look here, I *will* take the typewriter with me! So that you will get your ration occasionally ... on the old familiar type. What an admission! As if I hadn't got enough to cart about without a bloody old portable. But I will, promise you ... Of course in the letters which may come you will probably find a new me emerging. The working-one. I take it all rather seriously I'm afraid ... but I'll still be somewhere about ... not Friedrich Bruckmann entirely I hope ... and you must take comfort from the fact that I will, whatever happens, be happy because I am working again ... the reason that I am in such a bitch of a state financially now is that I have refused to work until the right work came along ... it has been a long wait sometimes ... but I whored too often in the past ...

38

The House

June 21st '68

I wasn't going to tell you this, but now that it is all over you may as well know ... when I wrote to you yesterday, as you will probably know before this reaches you, I was rather gritty and distrait. You will presently see why.

Last week-end I agreed to let someone come down to the house to look it over. You know it has been very discreetly on the market for some weeks? But, I insisted, only to a really important or serious buyer. I am in no hurry to leave here, and anyway all the summer plans may fall apart ... but if someone came who really wanted the house at the price I ask, and loved it as I did, I felt I could, possibly, be persuaded. Anyhow: a bit of a flurry on Friday night from my Estate Agent (v. grand and private) to say a Most Important Client, his capitals this time, was vastly interested, had unlimited loot, and was determined to see the house, could he come tomorrow? (Saturday.) Difficult, I had a full house party ... including Daph F. who was longing just to rest quietly. Anyway I said yes. My solicitors came down, tea was planned and, shortly before, a vast Rolls arrived with my Estate Agent [Bernard Walsh] and one Hammond Burton Wood. About fifty-five, shabbily dressed, open neck shirt, balding, wearing white sand shoes. He was also totally toothless. But had charming manners. I was a little taken aback, but was assured by Daph who knows about these things, or should, that really very grand people are a bit odd in their sartorial habits.

He made a tour of the house while we sat and wondered a bit, then came back to the drawing room, with a v. pleased looking Agent (!) and had tea. We talked about the Seychelles where he lived, and where he has an antiques business. He was very informative, and clearly adored the Islands where he has lived ever since the war ... knew a good deal about the flora and fauna and was pretty pleased with some of my paintings, and in particular the modest, but attractive, collection I have of Meissen wild birds ... tea was rather fun, and afterwards he asked me to take him round once again, and to see the land. Apparently security, he kept using the word, was essential.

So I went off with him. He patently adored the house, and confessed that it was not for him but for someone else. Who, he declined to say ... but did add that he had secured 'her' Town house earlier in the week from Lord B. and this was to be the 'country' retreat. He insisted on seeing all the Staff accommodation, inspected windows and doors, and was constantly glad that there were no neighbours and nothing was remotely overlooked, even made a swift check on the road approach to the house and the security of the garages! Anyway; after two hours, and a final detailed inspection of some of the porcelain and pictures (he picked up a pleasant Chinese bowl which stands in the middle hall, examined the mark, and was impressed enough to say, 'Ah yes ... I thought so! Exquisite!') ... they all left in their cars and we felt rather deflated. He said he'd give a decision within twenty-four hours, but had to refer everything to 'the lady in question'.

Daph, of course, said that he was a front man, that is to say someone doing the purchasing for a Very Important Person ... it quite often happened. Just before dinner the Agent rang in great excitement. I knew he was excited because he was strangely calm. The house was accepted, £150,000 plus contents! But minus all, or any, personal items which I particularly treasured ... and minus paintings. He had paid the same price for the B. house, was buying on behalf of a vastly rich woman, money being absolutely no object. There was a very strong hint that the lady in question was Royal. Hence the security and the privacy.

So that set the cat among the pigeons all through dinner. Daph, as ever the fount of Society Knowledge, suddenly said, 'I know! I bet it's for Fredericka of Greece ... she's looking over places in England. That's who it is!'

And I remembered that Mr Burton Wood had hinted, very gently, that the buyer was Foreign but spoke absolutely flawless English since she had attended a School here ... and was connected, he did not say how, with our Royal Family. So. Well you can imagine ... the next few days were spent deciding what and what not to take ... the offer was excellent, and it would save me storing so much ... if and when the time came to leave. Also, which was important, they were prepared to wait until the New Year to take possession ... as long as they could start work on re-fencing the entire property. They would come and do the Inventory on Thursday (yesterday). At eight-thirty a.m., precisely, yesterday morning, the Agent telephoned to say that Mr Burton Wood was a fake.

No one seems to know him, neither his solicitors, The Crown Office, nor Sothebys! The only people who *did* know about him were Scotland Yard who have booked him in to jug for many similar offences. He is perfectly harmless; likes having tea with the famous or the Gentry ... spends all his time in the prison libraries ... hence his knowledge of the Seychelles ... impeccable apparently because poor Lord B., who knows them well, was completely taken in! So I was not the only sucker ... I remembered his warm praise of the Chinese bowl in the middle hall, and went to have a look. In large red letters it stated simply, 'Made In China'. A splendid fantasy land ...

I dared not tell you, naturally, until things had been settled. I thought that, perhaps, you'd not mind me leaving here quite so much if it belonged to the ex-Queen of Greece! I don't know why. I suppose I thought that someone like that would care for it ... so we are back to square one. And no more awful alarums or excursions. The house remains mine, for the time being, and Mr Burton Wood is, as far as I know, sitting in his cell in Wormwood Scrubs. I must say: ten out of ten for trying! But don't please worry. I shall be very, very careful who buys 'our' house ... depend on that.

39

My letter of the 21st delivered 'after visiting hours'. So
we are back in the iron-bed department. Oh my dear!
Stitches and all the petit-point and gros-point to be fiddled
with: but perhaps this is really the clearing up department;
tidying up and getting you *really* well again?

... Your letter distressed me on two counts, the fact
that you are in physical pain again and also, due to me it
would seem, in mental pain as well. I wrote, as I did, only
to amuse you, to show you how idiotic I am and to prove
to you my gullibility; *not* to wound you. I will quote to
you what you may have forgotten you wrote: you say:

'Coup de grâce ... if you leave the house. The little fringes
of my heart that have never hurt when the whole heart ached,
now feel pain at the very thought of the house without you.
But ... c'est la vie ... and it helps me not care very much
whether the surgeon's knife slips on Thursday or not.'

And as if that was not enough to distress me you
continue:

'Except that you do (bless you!) make it feel as though our silly
literary amour could still go on ... even without our common
bond. But please don't cast me off with the house ...'

Christ almighty! What am I to do? Perhaps when you

wrote this from your bed you were terribly sad and appre-
hensive and fearful of pain and so on; I cannot believe
that you mean it seriously. The house was our bond ...
but only at the beginning surely? A house doesn't belong
to one for ever, does it? Oh yes, ancestral homes, that sort
of thing ... but *we* are only tenants of the things ... they
are ours only for as long as we can survive in them, and
when we find we no longer can, as in my case, and as in
yours all those years ago when because of impending war
you had to leave without a backward look, then we must
move on ... Life is what is important, living, loving,
being free to do those things ... when I leave the house
I shall not leave you ... I have promised and promised
you that. Surely, between the lines of this rubbish I write
almost daily, you realise that? Woman's intuition? Can't I
make you feel secure? Why distrust me? And you know,
it IS immoral of you, as you say, to suggest that I could
prostitute my soul (your words not mine) just a TINY
inch or so for the sake of the house! I cannot sacrifice my
career for a mere physical possession. It comes first of all
things in my life ... which is why I never married and
settled down and had a family and did all the perfectly
reasonable, ordinary, things in a well ordered life. I belong
to myself. I must be free at all times to do whatever I
consider right for myself. I want no permanent encum-
brances ...

But that does not include you: for you do not 'possess'
me at all! This is a particular friendship, and we must
cherish it as such or else it will become untenable for us
both. It has distressed me immeasurably to think that you
do not trust the particular affection I have for you, or the
hand, albeit metaphorical, which I put out to hold you in
your times of fear and pain.

I'm sorry. I bang on again. I am certain that when
this present unhappy phase is over, as soon it will be, you
will know that I am right, and you will be your usual,
bantering, wry, sendy-uppy self. But one thing must be

absolutely clear to you here and now. I leave when I leave. But all it will mean to you is a change of postmark ... and if you collected foreign stamps you'd be bloody lucky! So; belt up! Get well ... and give your Nurses and Doctors hell, not me ...

40

So it's tomorrow I leave. Sailing on *The Maid of Kent* ...
then the car on the train to Milan. I have been scuttering
about with last minute instructions to my Spaniards, and
Jim Grout (gardener) ... who is full of uneasy questions
because, as he says, three months or more is a long time
in a garden. Where do I want the cuttings of the Blush
China set out? Should he scythe the long grass down the
nut-walk or leave it until September? And did I get the
new lock for the door to the mower-shed. (I didn't.)

The suitcases are all about my bedroom ... heaps of
shirts and things everywhere. Shoes in tumbled piles.
What to pack for Rome, Essen, Paris, Düsseldorf, and
very probably Tunis as well ... for I can't see the chance
of a break between projects ... hope for one ... but don't
expect one and haven't dared tell the Staff yet that I may
not be back until January or even later. ... oh shit! I feel
wretched and very restless. I just want to get packed up
and on to the boat and go. Then the thing will have
started. It's the hanging about that is so awful. And
Candida knows what's up. Drooping about the house,
eyes hooped with mourning, snuffling at the suitcases.
Now at least I know what a hang-dog expression is ...

Now what? First of all how marvellous that the 'op' is
over and done with. And how I applaud your shining
courage. I wonder if I would be as brave? Don't want the
testing thanks. But don't be so potty: of course you won't

fall apart like a cracked lustre jug when the stitches come out. Far too strong for that. I reckon your poor silly head fell apart years ago, but the fabric on which they have done their fretwork and petit point and all the rest is far too tough ... even that fact percolates through your most whimpery-yallery-greenery-no-one-loves-me letters. Not, I must confess, that there have been many of those, and *then* with good excuses. I suppose, of course, that you ought to be careful about your first bath, though, don't you think? I mean what do stitches do in water? Melt? Can you imagine that? A slow melting and THEN you'd fall apart perhaps ... a sort of Francis Bacon. A silent scream ... one of those wiped figures he is so determined to explore. I did, I confess, rather long for one: a red abbot or cardinal or whatever they are. Difficult to hang. I bought, did I tell you, a Ben Nicholson instead ... madness. Cost a fortune (sold some stocks and shares) and won't be able to have it until September when the Show closes. And will it ever hang here I wonder? If not where, and when? Couldn't resist it ... it's an early work (1921) painted on board. My father looked very bewildered when he saw it. 'It isn't really your kind of thing at all,' he said doubtfully. I wonder what he thinks *is*? Anyway, it's mine.

... What else to amuse you, beguile the time and save you fiddling about with your stitches. (Of course they'll irritate.) Oh yes ... Jean [Smith] came down for the day last week. She's over with Eunice [Schriver] for the Tennis. They have both rallied extraordinarily well. Tremendously brave. But that family does have guts, they all seem to take after Mum. We avoided all the Security Guards, and she came down with an old school friend, and I cancelled the regulars for the week-end so that she could be alone. Which she was; we talked a lot about Bobby. She is very strong and calm. Seeing her sitting here in the sun, relaxed, laughing ... it was difficult to relate her to the wild and dishevelled creature in all the news photographs leaning over her dying brother in the

Ambassador kitchens only three weeks or so ago ... My
God! I SO admire that kind of courage and faith. I wish
I had it.

Yesterday a sort of farewell-lunch at Caroline Somer-
set's pretty house for her mum, Daph. Who, like you, is
just out of hospital and all stitched up and not feeling
terribly comfortable, but it was her sixty something birthday so she was determined to see it out. A pleasant cast
... Lords Plunket and Arran, Chiquita Astor who is v.
pretty, and Lady Arran who was gay and amusing. I was
very happy to meet *him* because he'd written a charming
letter to me a week or so before saying that a film I had
made ages ago, and which was considered rather daring
in its day [*Victim*] because it was about homosexuality,
had done a great deal to strengthen his fight to get his bill
through both Houses legalising homosexuality between
consenting adults. He was apparently much moved by it
... saw it on Telly as it happened ... and said that the
film had done a tremendous amount of good, and had
certainly helped to sway things in his favour. I was tremendously happy. That is why I did the thing in the first
place. I do think that the cinema can help to educate an
audience for *good* sometimes.

Patrick was pleasant, as indeed he always is, and said
that HM had enjoyed her luncheon that day ... rather as
if he had expected her not to. A faint echo of surprise
in his voice. Caroline says he bosses the Queen about
like anything; and she is just as scared of him as most
people are of their Staff who complain about too many
people for dinner ... I can well believe it. He was
very bossy with me when I tried to wriggle out of the
invitation.

After lunch all Daph's children came in ... Christopher
apparently none the worse for that idiot prank, and his
pretty wife, and Alexander Weymouth in a heavily em-
broidered coat from Afghanistan, covered with chains and
bangles and his hair in a bun. Rum lot the Thynnes. Daph

is the first to agree . . . all in all a happy, affectionate, family day. A pleasant way to say 'adieu' to London for a time.

When I got back a letter from Jean to say thanks for her 'no questions' day down here. She said it had completely relaxed her and she had felt very comforted and loved. As indeed she was, and is. Loved I mean. I asked her, that day, why she didn't start writing some kind of Journal . . . she has never kept any form of Diary at any time in her life: I said I thought it was almost a duty that she should. And she agreed. We talked at great length about writing, and I told her about you (without mentioning your name or where you were naturally), and she seemed surprised and moved too. She finally said that she thought she might try and do something on her mother. Which I fully encouraged . . . people need prodding!

Now I must prod myself up to the suitcases. I'll take up a bottle of Dom to help me. Or hinder. Depends. Remember I won't be able to write for a bit now . . . you won't be abandoned, you'll get the starlings as usual . . . just to keep in touch. But letters are out, I feel, until I see the road ahead. I am, truthfully, very scared. I have a hellishly difficult 'part' in the film, I'll be working with Italians and with a very demanding Master in Visconti . . . that I know. I simply must not fail this chance. I am at a sort of cross-road having chosen, after some deliberation, the road . . . but I can only guess where it will lead. There is, alas, no sign-post, no indication of what may lie ahead, or where I may end. If you aren't still plucking at the embroidery on your banjo . . . then place your fingers together and say a modest, but fervent, prayer for me. And if God doesn't know where I've got to, just add the address so that he can find me. I'm not far from his Town house as it happens. From July 14th it's the Hotel Hassler, Rome.

POSTCARD

Calais

July 13th '68

Crossed on *The Lord Warden*, calm, off first. Loaded car on Milan train, had excellent lunch here and train leaves at 3.15. Good to be moving again. Hated leaving but now am on way I only look ahead. Candida crumpled heap of accusatory despair, which hurt: but explain I have to earn money for her grub. No more room, but a mass of love as ever.

41

... and desperately, breathlessly, hot. Stuck here because, as usual, I am not needed (on the film) until they come back from shooting the sequences in Austria! Why not tell me ages ago? The usual muck-up. Costume fittings of course, and so on, but Visconti sitting in some Austrian lakeside village with a vast crowd of extras shooting the Night Of The Long Knives without, it appears, any money! Nothing changes. I spend the days trailing about in the heat, or driving out to Lake Bracciano which is cool and pleasant in a closed-in sort of way. Haven't seen it since '59 and it hasn't experienced the hideous building-boom of the city. Total ruin, filth, ugliness, sprawl every-where round Rome. What they have done here brings tears to one's eyes. Don't they *really* care? The London papers full of depressing news on the Czechoslovakia situation. The pressure from Russia grows: one is amazed and overwhelmed by the bravery of the Czechs who are refusing to bow to the Russian demands to cut their new liberalism, and who are standing out for freedom of choice. Who laughed at me, ages ago, for suggesting that the threat to democracy would come from the East? Well, perhaps it's on its way, my dear.

July 21st '68

Here for lunch [Porto Ercole]. Very self conscious plus dull food. Dainty; with 'don't pick' notices on all the wilting, unwatered plants in the twee garden. The Chaplins (Charles and Oona) with very pretty daughter and two unspeakable American film-types. She in tight pants, he with cigar and a voice to shatter granite. Conversation among them all about profit and loss and dollars. Boring. Could be Palm Springs...

Unterach

July 29th '68

First day's work all right. One shot only, which I did six different ways. Visconti seemed pleased, invited me to lunch. Honoured, I gathered. Tore here from Rome by car, exhausted. Decline offer tonight for *Don Giovanni*. Karajan conducting in Salzburg. V. *most* surprised, but I'm whacked. Are you well? Please be...

42

Hassler Hotel

August 20th '68

Home at last, the depressing German sequences all
finished. Don't bother with Düsseldorf or Unterach if you
get the chance. We bombed the shit out of the former and
the latter is so sickly-quaint on its little lake that one only
wants to throw up. Especially decked (for the film) in the
swastika and the red and black flags and everyone dressed
in dirndls or brown shirts and simply *loving* it! One
wretched Jew, driving through with his family apparently
on holiday, had a heart attack from shock, which caused
great merriment in the local pharmacy where we went for
help.

'All Jews kaput!' said a jolly, laughing blond, holding
her child high so that he could touch the flags.

The lamp of anti-semitism still burns as a beacon here.
And in the uniforms and flags the hysteria mounted. I felt
wretched: no one has learned anything except, perhaps,
the Jews who remain. No money for the film, the banks
refuse to lend us another lira, Visconti sits in his lovely
villa (via Salaria), tending his roses, and says that on no
account must we, the actors, return to the Studio until we
are paid. He leaves tomorrow for his summer villa at
Castelgandolfo, a rather sinister volcanic hole near the
Pope's house. I hate it. Depressing beyond belief. Sorry
to moan on, I think it is the heat, the German Episode,
and having no money and (and be good about this) a
telephone call from London from my loyal Estate Agent,

to say that the house has been snapped up at the asking price. I felt gutted rather. But it was the only sensible thing to do; after this epic is over I leave for Tunis, Paris and, perhaps, Los Angeles until well after Christmas ... and there is another film here in Rome after that. So there is no point now in owning a house in Sussex with a staff of four eating their heads off all on their own. I pray that this letter, the first you'll have got after days of starlings, won't reach you at a time when you are feeling wretched. One card from you here when I got in, wistful and sad and not altogether reassuring, but that was written on the 9th. Perhaps, and I pray it is so, you are getting to rights and maybe tomorrow I'll get a word from you full of greenery-yallery moans and hints which will make me laugh. I need laughter today. This is a rotten letter; I may not even send it...

43

Hassler Hotel

August 21st '68

At luncheon today, sitting in the courtyard under an umbrella, Mario from the bar came to the table, tears running down his cheeks, a little transistor in his hand. He set the radio on the table, weeping silently. Russia has invaded Czechoslovakia. We listened through the crackle and static to the BBC World Service and I translated for Mario and the now silent group of waiters who had gathered round us. One is appalled, even though somehow it was inevitable I suppose. Dubček has appealed for calm, and, as far as we could gather, there has been almost no resistance. Throughout the day, in dribs and drabs, we learned that Russia had been assisted by East Germany, Poland, Bulgaria and (shamefully) the Hungarians. What hope, what chance, could they have had in Prague? This evening we learn that Dubček and his entire cabinet are now 'in detention'. One's blood runs cold. The threat is now a fact, the frontier is not so far away, the tender blossoming of some kind of liberality has been brutally crushed by tanks. One feels near to tears, desolate. Useless.

There were two fat gentlemen from Texas sitting on the terrace at lunch. At least they looked Texan, white stetsons, paunches, pointed toes to their boots. They were patently irritated that there was, at that moment, no service, the waiters standing round my table, listening. They called angrily for two martinis, and other tourists started to drift in for lunch, paying no attention to the radio on my table at all ... probably didn't hear it.

One Texan said suddenly, 'What you seen this morning, Hank?'

Hank gave it some thought, he drank his martini, and then he said, 'I seen the Eiffel Tower. No big deal.'

The other man, after a silence, said, 'Couldn't have.'

Hank was calm, deliberate, slow. 'Saw the Eiffel Tower right down there in the square; Mae saw it too. I tell you...'

The other man finished his martini at a gulp. 'You were down in the Piazza del Popolo, that's where you said you were going, and there ain't no fucking Eiffel Tower there.'

'Well: we saw it. Ain't worth a row of beans.'

'It's in Paris, France.'

'We bin there?'

'Sure.'

'Ah. Want another drink? Mae and Diane'll have the same.'

But the Russians had crossed the frontier. That was more than a row of beans. No letter from you this a.m. ... perhaps tomorrow, the Italian mail is dreadful. If I do come here to live I'll have to buy some pigeons or something ... the lights are starring the indigo sky. The dome of St Peter's is pale almond green, there is a last streak of the day dying in a gash of crimson and the swifts are screaming about the belfrys of the Trinità ... it is so ordinary, so lovely: *how* lucky I am.

44

Hassler Hotel

September 11th '68

Still no money. On it goes. But, and this cheered me up, my goodness, another bundle of letters from you. And the typing was terrific! Such a relief to see that familiar yellow paper and the typewriting. No more titchy scribbles from that beastly Clinic place, or whatever it is. It means, at least, that you are home, and that you are sitting up and that Anna will be cherishing, and you'll be looking out at the September trees which you love so well and which I so detest. All that gold and crimson horribleness. Decay. Goodness! I AM glad that you are back and that the prognosis, as you call it, does not seem so dire. Patience I gather, loving care, rest, and countless starlings and bits of moan from me.

Dined with V. at his hideous Volcanic villa. Well; the villa is all right, but the situation is really creepy, one is utterly hemmed in and if some idiot said a great monster would surface from the still, leadened, crater below the terrace, I'd be not the least surprised. No wonder the Popes are so damned gloomy, looking out at this for their summer hols; it is as inspiring as an empty tomb.

But as you are on such a tiny diet, shall I drive you mad and tell you what we ate yesterday evening? Well; spaghetti en croûte with shrimps and black truffles, loup de mer, a delicious roast duck with thin green beans and a peach sorbet (fresh). There was wine, but I stayed with beer, to V.'s rather distant disapproval. He doesn't mind it in a café, but at his house it is apparently a reflection on his cellar. Bugger that. I hate getting pissed at big supper parties, although this was hardly a party, just five of us.

Visconti, after supper, talked of Callas and said that, apart from her gifts as an actress, in the grand manner of Bernhardt, she has a unique range of voice in an age when sopranos tend to be classified within a small span of octaves but she covers the field. He is assured (by her old teacher) that she is well able to return and sing *Traviata* which he's been asked to direct her in in Dallas, but he frankly doesn't see the point of going to Dallas and being shot. And they wouldn't appreciate it anyway. So it's a no-no.

Still no money for us. God knows why. And I have to report to Tunis for the Durrell film [*Justine*] on October 7th. V. says gloomily that I won't be finished, but we'll have to 'shoot' my bits when I get free from 20th Century-Fox. It is all madness. But he'll have a splendid time directing his protégé [Helmut Berger] and Ingrid [Thulin], there won't be anyone else left. The rest of us have other jobs. Oh! what a business this is. I AM so happy that you are wellish ... I'm going to re-read some of these sulphur-yellow pages again. Mind how you cross the road IF you do try a walk ... but don't move a step without Anna or B. ... to help you. Take it all nice and easy.

45

Can you believe? Money, finally, has been released and it seems that we may be able to continue with this wretched movie. Half the cast have cleared off to their various abodes, Munich, Milan, Paris, etc. and won't return until they are perfectly certain that they will be paid. Can't blame them. I have to clear off to Tunis on the 4th or about then. Leaving three weeks' work to do. V. very sad but resigned, what else. You'd HATE this profession, it is quite hopeless and cruel. How do I leave one film and report for another with one unfinished and the other pretty unspeakable? New script arrived via California for the poor Durrell film and one sits in despair. Four splendid books carved up and shoved into one ghastly muddle of a script. And I am committed. Oh dearie me.

But, and this is the really bad news for me, we now go to Hollywood after Tunis and not Paris. I gather that the Coast (the Studio) want to keep a beady eye on the Director and feel they can do it better if we are all safely under the umbrella of Los Angeles and its hideous suburbs. So Alexandria will now blossom on the back-lot at Twentieth, and get mixed in with bits of Tunis and the real 'Ayrab' desert, and I'll have to fly there directly, a long trip, and not see England for ages. Well, until next spring anyway.

I keep on trying to remind myself that I am doing all this for my old age, and that the money I shall be earning will go to helping me into a walking-frame, or having essential drip-feeds: you know what I mean. Silly of course. But one does rather think of 'time' now, and especially as you are constantly a reminder that wretchedness can overwhelm so suddenly. I was so happy to get the yellow letter paper and typing and so deeply unhappy when they turned, of a sudden, to the old note-book with lines and that familiar, beloved, but still dismaying scribble. Dismaying only, my dear, because it means that you are back in that place with the polished floors and the smell of ether. Oh shit! *Why* ...

Strangely, crossing the lobby this afternoon, back early from the Studio, I met Joseph Losey. Happily because he'd left a message for me which I had never been given ... Italia again. He's brown and well and miserable. Back from Sardinia where he has been on holiday. Is about to make another movie with Richard Burton which he now secretly, except he confessed it to me, dreads. They (the Burtons) do seem to behave pretty oddly and in a very cavalier manner. But he is, truthfully, very flattered that they court him. Can't think why. I'd run a mile from both. But they guarantee the money up front, if not at the box office, which is molto odd. And he and I, when we worked together, had to beg and scrape every cent to get anything made at all. Now he can have the world if he needs it, and they insist that they *do*. Yacht and all. Cartier watch and flowing champagne but not a great deal of talent on display. He, anyway, seemed reasonably resigned, and quite happy that he is their Director. Can't think what good it'll do him.

Got a bit pissed tonight at Fontenalla, which is noisy but where they know one and I got a quiet table, and discussed the difference between Losey and Visconti. A canyon.

I suggest, disloyally, that V. is a Giant and Losey is not quite. And feel rather wretched when I say so. Met by a thoughtful silence. No one committing at that stage. I try to analyse whether the background of knowledge and education, in its widest sense ultimately, if properly used, triumphs over the upward struggle. V. does appear to be hideously spoiled in that he simply won't do other than what he wants to do and is quite unconcerned over the consequences, but of course he can afford this materially I know, and it can't touch his core although I am aware that he is, actually, vulnerable through aspects of vanity. Losey's background, though not a poor one, as far as I can gather, is very much middle class middle America with a smattering of Jewish blood mixed in, although he insists he is, actually, of Scots descent. (Well ... Losey?) His outlook is cynical, Marxist, but a bit unstable. He'll dine with the Burtons on their yacht and watch Mrs B. feed the dogs caviar and think it 'amusing', and, as he says, after all is said and done, Burton 'was a miner'. I don't think that he got that *quite* right, but I sort of know what he means. He lived in a 'valley' near the pits: it'll do. But he absolutely lacks the core of inner confidence which V. so obviously has, and when someone said, rather shrilly, that V. would never 'understand the working classes like Losey', I was able to remind them of *Ossessione*, *Terra Trema* and *Rocco*, which rather shut them all up. I didn't win anything, I just felt disloyal. But Losey couldn't have touched those films with any degree of compassion or, more important, understanding. Why then, I wonder, still a bit pissed, can an arrogant aristocrat-communist? Education? Knowledge? I don't know. But I do know that I shall miss him most dreadfully when I go to Tunis. That won't be much fun, I feel in my bones already. I must chuck this and go to bed. The bells are clanging away somewhere: it *was* Saturday ... perhaps the Monks and Nuns are swinging about on the ropes already? I A M glad I decided not to be a Priest or something. All this rubbish to greet you in the linoleum-room. I'll write as soon as I know where I'll be. Write, if you are able, here. They'll keep them until I can send them the name of an hotel in Tunisia. Golly! Big deal ... be brave, be good and do just as you are told. *Please*...

46

... and therefore this must be a quickie. Thank you for
your reassuring note, I felt much better, and will contain
anxiety next time I write. But you DO worry a fellow.
And there seems to be so much to worry about, not just
about you and all, but about Europe and the tarrididdle
that seems to be taking place under our very noses. Helmut
[Griem] flew in from Munich today, an anxious chap. Says
the Germans are really pretty jittery about the Russian
threat that they feel themselves 'legally entitled to enter
Western Germany if the situation justifies it'. I seem to
have heard that phrase before, dear God! They are refer-
ring to the resurgence of the Nazis, or Nazism, at this
point. They'll use that as an excuse, so it is rumoured that
Bonn may have to ban the Nazi Party (I didn't know, in
all truth and ignorance, that it still existed. Officially. But
apparently ...) in order to show the world that a Russian
entry of German soil would, in fact, be invasion. Griem
seems to feel that things are more serious now than for a
long time, and filled me with gloom during dinner on the
roof of the hotel, a fairly gloomy business at the best of
times, apart from the amazing view of all Rome lying
below in a sort of casket of jewels at night. Gloomy, my
girl, merely because you can hear selections from *My Fair
Lady* and *The Sound of Music* a bit too often from a three
piece 'band' with a duff piano, awful food to please the
mostly American clientele: no garlic, a total lack of

oregano, but vast pepper grinders everywhere with which they smother their food without once savouring it: that, and the ketchup bottles on the tables, cast a sad gloom about the place, together with the definitive whine of the American female, complaining at pitch. All as rich as hell, solidly chewing their cud. I began tonight to wonder, sitting there among them, if another European war is not inevitable.

A plump chap at the next table said, in a loud voice, so that we should hear (he'd twigged we were European because I had complained about no garlic etc.), 'Well: if there is going to be a war, they can fuckin' get themselves out of it this time by themselves. Right? We won't lift a finger, not this time. No way.' There was great satisfaction in his voice.

Helmut and I switched to French instantly.

Heigh ho. I'm off to bed, leaving you with blankets of love. Snuggle up. Who knows what'll happen next?

47

You chide me, and of *course* you are right and I beg
forgiveness. I should not bleat away about the European
situation, or the awfulness of the visiting Americans, when
you are moaning away in your truckle bed and filled with
woe and despair. It is just that we are, of necessity, so
very far apart ... and I do get introverted (is that right
for what I am? That's what it feels like anyway) and I
should write about the daily idiocies: the flowers and the
date palms and the, what next?, camels and stench of 'pot'
and so on. Diverting things to beguile you. You know
what I mean?

All this because a fat package suddenly arrived from
Rome and there were your letters muddled up with the
electric light bill from England and Christmas Vicars and
their wives appealing for 'something personal' to auction
at their Christmas Bazaar. Christmas already! But your
letters, when sorted out and put in reading order (they
were all muddled up of course), put me clearly in the
picture; or as clearly as you're going to let me see, or
know.

But, the good thing, you are back under your chestnut
tree and home.

This constant coming and going must be devastating
for you, one moment in the linoleum-room, the next
heaved off back home. I am not altogether sure that you
ought to cart me along with you in my little green-frame.

I mean to the Clinic. The nurses will be fearfully rude, if they know who I am, and you suggest that they do because they have seen me on the TV doing those comedies which the British seem to be so famous for over on your side. We do make Grown Up movies as well. But not often.

Tunis is a sad place without the French. There are bits and pieces of them left still. Faded signs for Dubonnet painted on the sides of a house, the blue and white street signs, cafés with names like 'Chez Antoine' or 'L'Arc En Ciel' . . . They have torn down all the French memorials, and statues to the statesmen, and done all they can to eradicate the colonial past . . . but of course it still exists and it always will. The French were good colonisers, unlike the Dutch, and their influence goes deep: not least in the mixing of the blood. However.

I'll say nothing about the misery of the film, you've had enough of that in the last few weeks, enough to say that we struggle on and everyone is miserable. The other day the company flew in fifty Press people from all over America to watch the shooting. Put them all up at great expense, and chartered a vast plane. They all got Tunis-tummy within a day and were unstable to say the least, what with jet lag, the runs, and the Arab food which they dislike intensely. And at what cost! We have them for a week I fear.

Two very civilised people arrived from London to 'cover' us for *Vogue* (I think): Patrick Lichfield (a trendy, and v. pleasant, Lord 'doing' photography) and a ravishing creature called Kathleen Tynan. Married to the critic Kenneth Tynan, but I simply can't hold that against her, she is too much fun and together they are saving this disgraceful location with their laughter. We have found a pleasant little fish restaurant in Sidi-Bou-Saïd (where Gide had his house), a rather lovely Arab village, clean as a whistle, with white walls and blue doors (to keep off the evil eye) and it's quite near the d'Erlangers villa (which we are using in the film) which is simply breathtakingly beautiful, with great gardens tumbling down to the sea and a heart-catching view of Cap Bon away to the north. Anyway: Kathleen and Patrick, and anyone else who is half human on this film (and most are sub), go up there most evenings, to Sidi-Bou-Saïd I mean, and eat rouget and fat prawns and drink excellent wine and laugh and talk disgustingly about Nanny-Language. You know the stuff? 'Have we moved our you-know-whats this morning?' and 'Don't pick your nose and eat it or I'll shut you in the airing-cupboard.' Not funny... but on Tunisian red and a fat rouget, under the electric fan, we are crippled with mirth.

It is the rainy season now, it would be wouldn't it? So there isn't much beach life ... not that I have a day off anyway ... and the beach is crammed with the ugliest people you have ever seen, privileged Poles on a cruise, all playing volley ball and kicking each other in the shins ... the women! God! are vicious, in awful sort of knicker-things, with wobbling thighs, screaming in their gobbly language and laughing while they kick sand into anyone's face who happens to merely S I T on the beach, minding their own business. Odd lot.

POSTCARDS

Sidi-Bou-Saïd, Tunisia

October 22nd '68

In haste. Gide's house marked X on left. Kathleen and Patrick left for UK on Saturday, causing deep, blank, numbing gloom. No one now to laugh with. Weather ghastly. Eastbourne on a summer Sunday. Grey sea, bitter wind, heaving waves. Just eaten a huge couscous so feel swollen and grotty. Vile California looms. Postcards now order of the day. Je t'embrasse.

Hotel Abou Nawas
Gammarth, Tunisia

November 1st '68

Leaving tomorrow, thank God, for London, early flight. Needed in LA in a week's time so will see the house just once more, but do not give possession until New Year. Film almost total disaster. God knows what will happen in LA but we are in despair. Writing soonest from house. I will not miss Tunis one bit.

48

The House

November 4th '68

A first frost has put paid to the beastly dahlias which Mr
Grout plants with such relish, bless him. I really don't
think that they 'fit' in an English garden but would look
splendid in some dusty lane in Mexico. However: and so
one is now back, provisionally at least, while they settle
what happens to the film. (We are telephonically linked
every hour on the hour, except, of course, that we are not
because of the eight hour difference. Maddening.) But all
kinds of worrying messages fly across the Atlantic. What
is clear, however, is that there will be a change in the
Director and I have been told to hold on until required
to fly. It has been agreed, yesterday only, that if the deal
on the house goes through I must leave England for good.
Become an immigrant I suppose ... but can't quite make
up *where* I'll be an immigrant. Probably Italy because there
seems to be a constant stream of scripts from Roma, and
I'd quite like to work there and in any case I HAVE to
go back to finish off on *Götterdämmerung* for Visconti ...
he's waiting and impatient, but I've explained that I
haven't even started THIS epic yet. We will probably
have to re-shoot everything we have done in horrible old
Tunis. Oh Lord! the muddles! Anyway, Rome seems
probable. So harden your heart for me. I have to do what
is right for my work, and my senses tell me that I have to
clear out of the UK. Sentiment can't be considered. My
parents very understanding, Pa especially. 'If they don't

want you here, go where they do want you. Stands to reason.'

That makes sense to me even though it may shred a little of your heart at my leaving. I confess that I do look about me and wonder often. The view down the valley to the ghyll, the magpies tossing about in the magpie-tree, Hadlow Down hard against the sky, the lambs bleating in the meadow below the farmhouse. The smell of centuries of wood smoke in the panelling, the creak of the stairs going up to bed, the safety of merely being 'home' ... but that sort of sentimentality won't stand up today. I'd never be able to afford this, I am told, or was told yesterday by my 'advisers' one and all, if I stay. It'll all have to go in taxes and my future in the UK is bleak indeed. I mean, *one* Voice-Over for the timber industry is all I was asked to do ... and I did that damned commercial (for a heap of dollars) in Rome that time because there was simply nothing else and I felt it might be a sprat to catch a mackerel, so to speak. It was. I met Visconti, got the Durrell script, and another ahead ... so ... it seems right and sensible; please think so with me? You will never be 'cast off with the house' as you once said, *never that*. You'll just have to put up with another sort of house, and God only knows what, or where, that'll be. Trust me ... I have to trust myself. Not easy for someone who is accused of being 'mercurial'.

I'm off now for a beer downstairs, and Antonia has just brought in a big bunch of catkins (early?) which I reckon I'll never see in full pollen ... be on the plane by that time; or maybe she's going to lay the fire? Could be ...

49

Connaught Hotel, London

November 8th '68

Sorry about scribbly writing. Thin nibbed pen, and Adler [typewriter] all packed up. We leave tomorrow for LA on Pan Am 121 which is supposed to be coming from Paris. I only hope that it does: we go over the Pole. Quicker I gather, and tonight I am host at my last supper here for a while. The Loseys, Kathleen Tynan, Robin Fox and Boaty Boatwright from the Deep South. The invaluable Arnold has telephoned me from LA (he flew ahead from Paris) to say that things are '*mildly* well organised' but that I'll see some changes. Wouldn't elaborate on the telephone, but says my accommodation at the Beverly Hills, Bungalow 3, is fine and the Montands [Yves Montand and Simone Signoret] are 'right next door'. Well, that's something; old and loved friends at least to cheer me in what is bound to be a forlorn and disturbing new existence.

Off to change for supper; remember how much you are loved too. These notes should be proof of something, surely? Apart from illiteracy.

50

Bungalow 3
Beverly Hills Hotel
Los Angeles

December 25th '68

It's been a funny sort of day: not like Christmas really at all. Probably because it has been warm, wet and miserable generally. But mainly, I reckon, because this is about the first Christmas when I have had absolutely NO responsibility at all. Refreshing? Just pottered about this faintly gloomy bungalow, visited chums in a sodden canyon, went up to tea with splendid George [Cukor] who was surrounded by his imported European-Elegance, and very nice it is too after the tat and trash of the rest of LA. But there was no turkey, no cracker, no wrapping of unwanted gifts (thank God) and for almost as long as I can remember my beloved Pa didn't make his annual speech, or toast rather, after dinner. The one that always made everyone deeply sentimental, but which he insisted on making, was to tell us all that this was a time for 'stock-taking' and that we should drink to absent friends ... casting, therefore, a suitable Dickensian gloom over us all. But he meant well, bless his heart. So here I am banging away at this before going on to someone else's place for drinks ... not Christmas Dinner ... they have taken pity on the 'lonely British' I think; kind but misplaced. One is not lonely and the husband is desperately aggressive and the children tiresome and she's a bit of a drag too. Talks far too much. But it's a kind thought.

Writing about 'stock-taking' brings to mind the number of things which have taken place in this lopsided year: the

Roman Venture which still waits to be finished, the misery of Tunisia, the arrival here at this funny little house buried in banana and hibiscus and tall palms. White clap-board and a fretwork verandah, although you-all call it a porch, I gather, and the struggle to get poor old Durrell put together again after the appalling scripts which got shoved before us. Thank heaven Cukor was the replacement. At least he had a full knowledge of the *Quartet* and did his best, with help from students from UCLA, to restore to the characters most of Durrell's original, and excellent, dialogue. But it's all been pretty fraught, and I'll not bother you with any more. I am sad that there has been so little time for real letters, you have been good, not whimpering and accepting the starlings without complaint. As far as I know!

The bungalow has been pretty well filled with chums all the time: Simone and Yves are next door, and Ingrid [Bergman] moved in next to them as I told you, and people seemed to be 'dropping in' most of the time. Which is, it appears, perfectly normal in LA in this transit-hotel.

But, really, above all, you have been so patient and so brave. Not a single moan from you, but a constant, and wondrous cheering, flow of lovely yellow paper ... it has kept the bond gloriously alive, and I have felt wretched that all you get in return are postcards of Sunset Boulevard, Graumans Chinese Theatre, or sunsets over Malibu. I've practically run out of cards! The girl at the Drugstore near Rodeo Drive is my friend now, but fails to find NEW views. We've used them all up.

I confess, because it's Christmas Day, that I *have* been tempted to pick up the telephone from time to time. It seemed so much easier than writing these tacky cards; but I resisted. A promise is a promise, a pact a pact. We are the people of the letters, and ever shall remain. But it has been sometimes a terrific temptation. However; I overcame the urge. Anyway, soon all this will be in the past, I'll be back in England, packing up the house, and

going away to Italy . . . where I reckon I'll stay for a while.
My good Antonia and Eduardo have agreed to chuck
England too and come with me even though I will not
be able to pay them a weekly wage owing to the fact that
I'll have almost no money once I start to emigrate. I think
that I'm allowed five thousand pounds only [by HM
Gov.] which won't go far. However, I shall pay them in
England for the year in advance, and give them pocket
money in Italy. This suits them very well, because they
can now put down a lump deposit on a flat in Valencia so
that, when the time comes, they will have somewhere to
retire to. It all *seems* neat and tidy. We'll see if it works.
The THEORY is fine. But then all my blasted theories
sound fine until put to the test. Maybe they won't be able
to stick out the year. Maybe they'll go back to Spain and
start a family: I know that is Antonia's idea . . . anyway,
we'll leave it and hope for the best. Hoping for the worst
is so unhealthy.

Something which I didn't, couldn't, put on a card . . .
and there is so much that one can't, was a strangely
moving moment when Jean [Kennedy Smith] came out
to stay for a week. She had gone to Mass and came over
to my bungalow rather depressed one day to say, simply,
that she had had a 'sudden vision' that Edward (her last
brother) was running for President and was shot before
her eyes. It distressed her greatly; with reason. She
wouldn't be reassured that pressure, and strain, had
produced a sort-of nightmare in the daylight. 'There is a
curse on the family,' she said with perfect control and
simplicity. 'Something terrible is still in store for us.' I
was miserable too. What more *can* they suffer, for God's
sake?

She admitted that it was a 'flash thing', faded almost as
soon as she had raised her eyes. But we both felt wretched.
Not improved by my nice Polish, or Hungarian, not sure
which, maid who arrived with a gigantic Christmas tree,
all covered in fake frost and red glass bobbles. Not ours,

no one ordered anything, I loathe Christmas and its trees (especially 'frost foamed'), but told her to put it in the sitting room. She was cooing and bleating like a demented pigeon. Awful thing. There was no card, so I don't know where the hell it came from, but some rich fillum-star, or An Other, has lost a hideous present and I've got it sitting in a corner of the sitting room behind the eucalyptus-log fire-place. Sort-of fake, with gas burners. But cheerful. Wasn't it sad about J. [Jean]?

A funny old time altogether in California.

Last night watching the first men to go round the moon, on TV (there are a few, very few, times when TV is exciting), was a sort of agony for about ten minutes. They disappeared from sight trying to fire their motor to get out of the orbit of the moon. It was the most extraordinary feeling of terror mixed with helplessness. Did you watch on the East Coast? Extraordinary. And then as they came round from the far side we could hear, quite distinctly, one of the blokes say, 'Let it be known that Santa DOES exist.'

An unforgettable moment, deeply moving, and a great achievement for your adopted land. How proud they must feel, and do, I suppose, in between the parties and 'Jingle Bells' and the pink-painted reindeer at the end of Sunset.

But perhaps the release of the captives from the *Pueblo* was more popular. Certainly it was more vulgar. A thoroughly disgraceful business altogether. But I'm glad that Santa Claus DOES exist!

Most dear girl: this is the longest letter you have had in ages. I apologise. But today is a sort of non-day ... and I know just how much you loathe the Festive Season; even more than me. But I wanted to be in touch with you anyway, and I have time in this funny little bungalow sitting at the dining table in the gloom with that filthy tree glittering scarlet bobbles and spiked with foam-frost and bows glowering at me from the corner. Honestly, the sooner I get out of here and back to Europe the better:

we simply *don't* mix, and I can't 'play the game', which is idiotic because if I could, by tearing off to parties and sucking up to VIPs in the Polo Lounge, I might make some money, which would be useful. But as I keep my watch on English time always, there doesn't seem much hope for me. Heigh ho. Now off to Mulholland Drive and the evening's entertainment. Pistachio nuts, double-strength vodka and rather a lot of Indian Art from Santa Fe. Golly.

51

Bungalow 3
Beverly Hills Hotel
Los Angeles

January 23rd '69

It's all over. The bungalow stripped out, still gloomy, packing finished, leave in a few hours on Air France 707: Europe at last! Writing this before I strap up poor battered Adler. Bought yards of sticky yellow tape to wrap round him and hold him together. Alan J. Lerner and Karen, his wife, and Yves and Simone coming in for farewell drinks at six. So I must get this off the table and wrapped up. Just wanted you to be aware that I'm aware that you are sitting in your little salon with its pot-belly and knowing that I am on my way again, or you are presently asleep I suppose? And hope, and I must get myself together and face the torrential rain. I pray we don't crash on take-off. Never have liked flying and hate it in adverse weather. But I'll write again when I get to London and after I have dealt with the house. From the look of things I won't have much time. Straight on to Rome as soon as the dust has settled. Then to Spoleto, of all places, because we have to work in some vast steel works in Terni. This is for the Visconti Epic, have to report there by the 29th, so you will see it's all a bit of a rush. Don't write until *after* that date, and then when you do (if you do that is), write to the Hassler Hotel, for I will use that as my post-office at least until I find lodgings. But fear not: you will not be out of my mind and if I can I'll shove off the 'starlings' as often as time permits. Do you realise that we have started another year together? Corks! Well, well.

And you thought that this would be just a temporary little 'affaire'. It's been better than that so far. You really are a bit soppy sometimes; but hang on in there girl, we may make another year.

I'm off into the rain. With endless love.

Villa Fratelli
via Manfredonia
Roma

March 18th '69

You will have to excuse the paper and all the rest. I'm
not nearly settled down for letter writing, or sorted
out yet. But at least I have a house, of sorts, and an
address now, so I feel less like a wandering minstrel than
I did.

Everything is very Italian of course. In the house. I've
rented it for a year and got a slight reduction on the terms.
But there are not enough blankets, two miserable table
lamps, some tin knives and forks, ashtrays pinched from
hotels, bars and restaurants here and there. Mattresses
covered in pee-stains. *So* comforting. It was leased to an
American family in N A T O I gather, hence the muck and
the abandoned animals. Two cats and a small, starving,
dog with sores and a smashed fore-leg. Apparently the
N A T O family had six children and bought them the
animals as presents but dumped them when they had to
return to the States. So says the agent-lady in Rome. She
said I could drown them easily. Well: I could I guess.
There is a resident gardener, very aged, but probably only
forty, who tends a patch behind the house and grows
things. He says.

We are about twelve kilometres from the City, on a hill
with terrific views over the village rubbish dump and the
scatter of little villages in the plain below which are all,
really, suburbs of Rome. Square huts built of tufa blocks,
mud roads, lots of telly aerials and vast refrigerators

standing in the front yards attached to the electric light cable running overhead. Madness.

But the mountains are still there, and the pines, I am surrounded by umbrella pine trees, smell wonderful, great mimosa bushes toss golden rain over huge veils of violets thrown beneath their shade. Real Parma ones, the ones you love, and they smell amazing in the rain. And it rains daily I might tell you.

Got a swimming pool. Presently full of pine needles, but I reckon we can clear them one day, give me something to do. I sleep in a small room with pheasants on the wallpaper, a wooden chandelier, in a titchy four-poster with 'Bloomingdale's' stamped on the head board (at the back, of course). The widow who owns the house loved America so much that she brought the wallpaper, most of the furnishings (fake American Colonial stuff) and curtain material back with her. Which seems rather a pity.

Everything comes from Macy's or Korvett ... the furniture from Bloomingdale's as stated. Only the mattresses, alas!, come from Italy. Skinny things, straw filled on wire frames. We'll have to do something about that. Antonia and Eduardo are in a large bed-sitter on the top floor with a nice little terrace and a lovely view all the way to Frascati. They arrived pale and weary from Valencia on Friday evening and we all hastened back here from the awful airport.

I, naturally, couldn't resist the starving puppy and much against my better sense adopted it gingerly into the kitchen with some dog biscuits. Peppino, the aged gardener, kept roaring in and kicking it out into the garden or else chucking it over the high gate into the road, but it always managed to get back in, shattered fore-leg included. Determined. As it was accustomed to this house once, poor beast, I suppose it's certain it'll be welcome. Riddled with worms, like ropes of old spaghetti. Anyway, before I went off to meet the plane from Valencia, I fed it well and the result of my lavishness was apparent in the air the instant

I opened the front door. The stench was appalling. And it was EVERYWHERE, hall, stairs, sitting-room, all over. We were gagging, our feet skidding. A ghastly arrival for two air-sick Spaniards. I was on hands and knees for hours, sloshing bottles of carbolic everywhere which I found in a shed by the garage. I *think* it was carbolic: it stank like it and burned a hole in my shirt.

The dog? He sat watching with enormous brown eyes and a golden coat. He has pricked ears and a long slender tail. Looks like the dogs on the frescoes in Pompeii ... and is apparently a 'hill-dog'. That means he's wild.

Okay. I'll take him on. And get him to a vet as soon as possible ... the worms really are anti-social and the leg is smashed in three places. I bet Peppino hit him with an iron bar; either that or he was struck by a car ... whatever; he's called Labo, and stays. Idiot that I am.

53

Villa Fratelli
via Manfredonia
Roma

April 3rd '69

Elizabeth has arrived for a couple of weeks. Was going to bring Candida out with her but we all decided that it would be too cruel to lock her in a cage and fly her all the way out as freight. She's nine after all; and happy enough with Elizabeth's family who love her. So. Antonia blanched at the news and sobbed for a little: but that really is, I think, because she is absolutely terrified of the Mafia. Convinced that they hide under every oleander, mimosa, rose, or even behind the chicken run. Especially to get her.

Maybe they do. God knows. But she's convinced; almost convinces me. It's quite a lonely villa after all.

What idiots we are, really. Not a word of Italian and running a not so small house with hardly any money. I find the supermarket rather fun. Never been in one before. This one, Super Romano, is terrific. I rattle about with my trolley and buy everything in sight. The car becomes loaded with an amazing tumble of diverse objects. Tide, candles, dog-food, a cutting board, lavatory paper, brush for the hearth, carrots and black olives, cheese and four dozen eggs, Martell and a turkey feather duster thing.

That was today's list anyway. And I bought a vile looking cactus four foot tall covered in warts and needles. The manager said I could have it cheap because I had spent so much. Which frightened the wits out of me. I've only been here a few weeks, and 'so much' simply won't do. No more cactus.

Thank goodness that the Italian government 'froze' half of my salary here. I was enraged at first naturally, but now see the wisdom of it ... I must spend it all here, and as I am an 'immigrant' with a limited amount of money from our generous Government in the UK, it is most useful. I've got a dog and Antonia has adopted three cats, Tiger, Prune (for rather obvious reasons I'm afraid) and Putana, a real tart from the village. Prune stinks. So we'll probably have to have 'them' off. Labo has been wormed and put into plaster. And that didn't cost nothing. The vet was horrified that I had collected a wild dog and was prepared to spend money on mending it. His wife, the vet's, was about to have an operation for cancer that week. We did a deal. I paid for her Op. and he mends the dog. Seemed sensible. Agree?

But I think that I'll quite like living in Italy once I get over the hump of idleness. I've never done nothing before, and it is a bit worrying. I tend to sit about drinking Frascati and sighing. Odd. So I've pulled myself together and got down to writing this; it's important that my mind doesn't atrophy completely ... but I am SO tired. I've been on the run, it seems, for so long. Budapest, Tunis, Rome, LA and clearing up the house.

I know what you mean in your letter of the other day, my 'birthday letter', that now is the time for me to start seriously to work at my syntax and spelling and all the rest and 'write properly'.

My dear; I *can't* write properly. I don't even know what a noun is. Adverbs could be sardines for all I know, you say I use both 'in netfulls' ... and I like adjectives *very much*, so there we are. I got into bad habits years ago and, if you recall, I hit 48 on the 28th of last month, too late to teach an old dog and so on. If I tried to punctuate properly you'd fall off your seat and bust your stitches.

And that won't do at all. But gosh, you are a bully ...
really.

54

Villa Fratelli
via Manfredonia
Roma

April 23rd '69

Got in from the vet. Rabies injections and so on, and a check of the plaster cast, the vet being very kind indeed now that he realises that I have lost my heart to this Pompeian hilldog. But the most important thing is that I have rented, from a rather curious English girl down in the flea-market, a mass of old junk furniture. She imports truck loads of Victorian rubbish from England, does it up and flogs it. Got some side tables, chairs, three chests of drawers (what do the Italians do with their shirts and knickers I ask you? Not one single piece in this Villa). But! Perhaps best of all, a DESK! With torn leather top and five drawers on each side and a swivel chair to sit in. It is now on the little terrace outside my bedroom with a splendid view over the trees, the village, to the via Fla-minia (in process of being built by the noise) . . . but I can write there without Antonia washing round my feet as she is constantly doing. The dog sheds hairs on the tiled floor, it's a rather repellent burgundy colour, so they show up and she gets fussed. But she'll stay clear of my terrace, she has promised. So here I sit. Adler on his desk, my backside in a chair, and I bought a stack of onion-skin paper (cheap for air-mail) and I'll write you something jammed with verbs and split infinitives and adjectives and all that jazz: and you can correct them for me, and mail them back as 'examples'. *Won't* we have fun?
   The view is nice anyway:

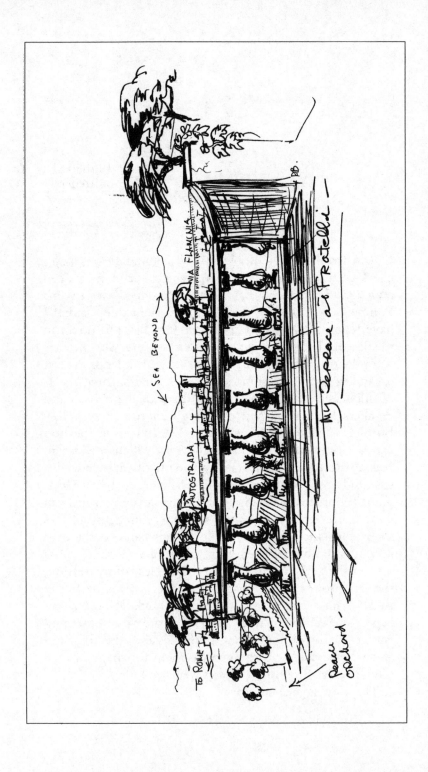

55

Villa Fratelli
via Manfredonia
Roma

Ascension Day
May 15th '69

The heat rises, one's arms stick to the papers on the desk,
sweat dribbles down one's forehead. It's foul frankly. And
today is another ruddy holiday ... I can't imagine how
Italy gets run, every second day is a Saint's Day. They are
never off their knees and EVERYTHING closes. I
tried a bit of gardening, spraying the evil greenfly, picked
a few roses but they fall to pieces in the heat before I can
get them into Antonia's kitchen, so I came up to my room
which is marginally cooler, especially on my terrace, and
looked at the abandoned bookcase here. I rather *overlooked*
it; it's just wooden planks and a few rows of tattered
books left behind by the NATO people. She scrawled
her name on every fly-leaf, in that odd, spidery, American-
Standard-Writing-hand. Like looped fuse wire. They seem
to be dated 1935 up to the '40's ... a very catholic collection. *Little Women*, of course, *How To Landscape Your Home*
by Malkin, *The American Twins Of 1812* (What CAN that
be!) by Lucy Fitch Perkins, *Adventures With A Lamp* by
Ruth Louise Partridge, and *You Must Relax*, in its third
edition, by Machonichie.

Now how about all that? Lots more, but these seem
typical ... bet you haven't got that little lot in your ivy-
covered library! I did, however, find *The Weather in the
Streets* (Lehmann) which I read ages ago and loved and
will read again, and an odd book by someone called Vidal.
American, of course, *The Fall Of Valor*, mixed up with

179

two or three 'collected' works of Dickens and Trollope
... so there is a bit for me to be going on with. And you
suggest that *I* should write! With all this junk tempting
me away from my Italian grammar. Trouble with Italian
is that it IS so grammary. I'll never get the hang of it,
and I can't find it in my heart to love a language which
contains 'Scusi' for 'I beg your pardon'. So *simpering*.
English is bad enough with your bullying ... I'll use deaf
and dumb language, not easy, but I bet you can't split an
infinitive by hand. Can you?

Forgive this idiot scrawl. Heat, Holiday, Homesickness
suddenly. But *that* won't do. The past is the past, all
finished. And nostalgia is a killer.

My devotion, as ever, and don't get *too* grumpy with
me. I am trying my best. Honest.

56

Rome in August is not a whole heap of fun. I think of you often sitting in the shade of your chestnut tree, cool at least. Even in the shade here one is wringing wet which is tiresome and doesn't make one feel a bit engaging.

But there have been compensations in the heat. Visconti came to lunch with his adorable cousin Ida, not so much to see me as to eat vast helpings of Antonia's English trifle which he likes above all else. But during lunch he chucked a small packet across to me, wrapped in gold and black paper, and said it was a present for my cut-to-ribbons performance in *Götterdämmerung*.

It was the Penguin edition of *Death in Venice* and he says that I can play Von Aschenbach, and we'll start in early spring next year before the tourists really hit Venice. I feel rather weak at the knees. Wouldn't you? He says I am *not* too young, which is something I worried about, and he is basing it on the fact that Thomas Mann based the part on Gustav Mahler whom he once met on a train from Venice to Munich covered in make-up and sorely distressed by the fact that he had 'seen ultimate beauty' and had nothing else to do but die. All a bit confusing to my idiot mind. Anyway, he's using Mahler's music and has instructed me to buy every record I can and to play it until I go mad. I probably will too. My musical taste, while not exactly *Lilac Time* or even *Showboat*, is still limited. I'm not at all certain about Mister Mahler, but

181

then hardly anyone I have spoken to this week has *heard* of him.

Well. There's a job offered. Pleasing. And today, can you believe?, a quite unexpected call from Alain Resnais from, of all places, the Tunis Hilton. He said he wanted to come and see me to talk about 'a lovely project', but wouldn't say what. So I become very immodest indeed. Well, my girl, think on it. Losey, Cukor, Visconti, Clayton, Schlesinger, Renoir and now Resnais. No actor could receive greater praise than that, to be asked for by them all. Gone to my head, it has. And if I had stayed on in the UK I'd probably still be doing Voice-Overs for the timber industry or Babycham. Goodness! I am glad I took that advice and cleared off when I did. But what I need now is a nice little job paid in lira. We are getting a bit low it seems, and I DO try to economise. But somehow it melts away rather alarmingly ... and the Visconti film *may* go in early spring and the Resnais 'lovely project' won't be until the *end* of the summer, that I know ... so something soonish will help feed us all. We have twenty ruddy pullets which Peppino smuggled into the hen run ... scrawny things, and Labo lies outside the wire dribbling with lust. O Lor' ...

57

Villa Fratelli
via Manfredonia
Roma

September 26th '69

Golden weather: up in the eighties, and I have a foul cold. But here you are: I have done my best, at your command, to 'force memory' as you said, and write about those halcyon days of childhood in Sussex so many years ago.

I don't know what it's like; I mean I LIKE it, I think there is a flow to it, or to the three chapters (rather short I agree) which I hope, the mail allowing, you are presently holding in your hot little hands. It's called, for the time being, *The Canary Cage** ... may not stay at that, but for a working title it'll do. It's symbolic of the sort of canary-cage existence we lived in during that decade from '25 to about '36 ... can't be absolutely certain of the exact years and have none of my diaries or notebooks here in Italy. Everything is in store in Angleterre. Now: I *have* done my best with nouns and verbs and all the things you dislike and say I scatter about like confetti ... but because, as you say, I am 'iggorant' you'll have to put up with things as they are. I spent rather a long time at this tattered desk on the balcony trying to re-live, for you, my past. An odd feeling. Once I had started all manner of names and places, smells, and views, came rustling back. Things I really did think I had forgotten. To such an extent that I even managed to telephone Elizabeth, no mean feat here where automatic dialling is a novelty still, to check things out with her. Women have better memories I reckon: at least

* This finally became *A Postillion Struck By Lightning*.   D.B.

for the trivia of life which give it such depth. And she in turn telephoned our 'nanny', Lally, who was a mine of information and a great help.

So. What you are about to read, if you still are capable in that wretched Clinic-place (why there again? How long for? Is there pain still? So many questions. *Don't* answer until you get back to the house. *Please don't.*), what you will read is as near accurate as possible. I just hope it's not too 'sicky' ... childhood can be: and it DID always seem to be summer. Anyway I send this with my love and to perhaps divert you in that linoleum-room for half an hour. I have used 'dots' where I couldn't work out if I should have used a comma, a semi-colon, or a whatever-you-call-them. I don't know all the names yet ... but did manage to buy a *Roget's Thesaurus* in the Red Lion Book Shop in town [Rome] last week, so I am gradually finding alternative words. Rather fun ... and a relief for the reader. Difficult to use, isn't it? And I always thought that he was Frog, but he's English I gather. Goodness, I'm learning things every day ...

POSTCARDS

Villa Fratelli
via Manfredonia
Roma

October 20th '69

Off to Florence and Montecatini and lunch with the Tynans, will look at some houses in Tuscany. Maybe it's cheaper there. Can I live in Italy I wonder? The day is mellow, yellow, fading leaves, mists, blackbirds chuck-chucking. How I hate autumn. Off I go, car waiting. Love . . .

La Colombe d'Or
St Paul de Vence
A.M.

November 11th '69

Trailed around this area (Grasse) for ten days looking at various obscenities all too expensive. But HAVE found the house I must HAVE. Half derelict shepherd's house up a hill in olive groves. A view to the sea which wrenches the heart. Snags commence. Money from UK! Must make offer soonest! Back to Rome in an hour. Write longer from there.

58

Villa Fratelli
via Manfredonia
Roma

January 11th '70

Life is coming back to normal after the misery of Christmas. Shops open and I can mail this off to you. Huge supper party at Visconti's on New Year's Eve which was fun in a way; I had no Italian of course, and everyone shrieking at each other and jangling their bracelets, men and women. Vast tree, presents and acres of food and cellars of champagne. So I am a bit wonky today still.

The documentary (*Upon This Rock*) was finished on time after all, and we were out of God's Town House at the appointed time (St Peter's) which was a relief to one and all. It was a marvellous experience, and I would not have missed it for anything. In spite of the aching cold. But it was a tremendous honour to be permitted, by the Pope, to film there at all. We were carefully vetted, I gather, Ralph Richardson, Dame Edith Evans, Orson Welles and me. All passed the Pope's strict rules ... EXCEPT poor Orson Welles! Divorced or something. Anyway I read his 'bits' and Richardson read James 1st, and Dame Edith the letters of Queen Christina of Sweden. I did Manzù and the diaries of Michelangelo plus letters from Bonny Prince Charlie. They are all buried in the basilica which is why we were there. But we were forbidden to wear make-up, evening dress, or to look at each other or be 'shot' together at any time. Rather daunting. But we managed. Edith was quite magnificent in long black velvet and pearls, her hair beautifully groomed, white and soft. We had not met since I was in a show with her in London just before I was called up [*Diversion II*]. She called me 'the little black thing'. Kindly. Hearing her glorious voice soaring up into the shadows of that amazing church was breathtaking. Absolutely. There were only eight Crew Members allowed, the three players, and a *lot* of policemen. The first night (we 'shot' for three) was rather grim in that no woman, I was told, had ever set foot in St Peter's after sunset. Not even a nun! So Edith can claim to be the first woman ever ... I tried to smuggle Antonia in, she was breathless with joy but we got discovered, alas. However, after the first night the police got bored and all curled up behind the high altar with their guns and went to sleep. I could have walked out with any treasure I could have pocketed. Amazing.

Richardson was pretty splendid, too, and I got through the Prince and Manzù (he created the great bronze doors, quite spellbinding) ... Edith was so good, which they had not expected her to be, she is, after all, in her eighties and had a hell of a lot to say, but she finished her 'bit' in one evening and was furious! She had never been to Rome and simply longed to look about, but was to fly back to London next day. Silly girl. Her main dream was that she could visit the tomb of Little John. The most adored of all the Popes, he was so honest, warm and funny, and it is still rumoured, in the blacker parts of Rome, that he was 'dealt with'. Could it be possibly true? I'd not be surprised really, the Vatican is a very scary place altogether, and apparently Pope 23 was resented because he was basically a peasant and the people worshipped him. It is equally rumoured that he used to steal away from the Vatican and was often to be seen freely in the streets, but I expect that is not so. Anyway, Edith wanted to pay her respects to his tomb, and laid the charge at my door! I can't think why. At the supper in a small trattoria, tiled floor, strip lighting, juke box, Espresso hissing away and a large mural of a lake weeping with wisteria, she asked me to ask the Chief of Police of all Rome to let her go down to the catacombs. The Chief of Police was a stocky gentleman, military cap, black glasses, gun at his hip, leather jerkin, boots and breeches and a face as graven and cold as a dead hake. My Italian was pretty duff, but I managed to stammer out what I wanted. (Isn't it strange that, confronted with a senior policeman of this kind, one is immediately guilty of a thousand offences?) He looked at Edith, Royal as an Empress in her velvet and pearls and a rather good mink coat, conferred with a couple of thugs similarly dressed as himself, and with a surly nod of his head indicated that the trip was on! I was amazed.

Edith was perfectly calm, and when I told her that it was a very long walk down a million stone steps and then through the top layer of the ancient city which stood *under* the Church, she shrugged and said she was a 'country woman'. So down we went ... In the strange, silent, world of dead Popes, all save a couple or so are buried here from the start of time, shadows leapt and feet echoed and the only light came from single electric lamp bulbs hanging from wires in the centre of the arched tombs stretching into infinity.

Pope John's tomb, the most recent, was, however, brilliant with candlelight. Massed with flowers, with votive offerings of various kinds, with supplications scribbled on bits of paper, old photographs of the dead or the dying, and he lay, or his stone image lay, arms crossed, eyes closed, smothered in carnations and roses and tiny bunches of dying violets. It was very moving. There was a wooden barrier to prevent the hysterical from going too near, but obviously people had done so, for their offerings and prayers were abundantly displayed upon the tomb.

Suddenly the Chief of Police leant across the barrier, took a carnation from a large bunch which someone had laid at the Pope's feet, and, touching the stone forehead with the flower, like a wand, he turned and offered it to Edith with the greatest reverence. She was standing absolutely still in her mink, her hands joined in some sort of prayer. It was a glorious sight, this ageing woman, straight-backed, regal, a splendour in black. I thought that was that, and we could start the terrible climb to the top again ... but Edith did something very strange. Standing perfectly still, she suddenly shrugged off her mink coat with no perceptible movement, so that it fell at her feet, and stretching out her white arms she said, 'I wish to embrace him.' For a shocked moment I thought she must mean the Chief of Police. So, I think, did he ... we stood in mute surprise watching her. Clearly she meant Pope John. I whispered to the Chief of Police. He looked at me with astonishment, and then at Edith holding her carnation, and then, to my amazement, he opened the wooden barrier and motioned her to enter. She lay, this extremely elegant woman in long black velvet, across the effigy of Pope John, her arms embracing him, her face pressed close to his stone throat, and all that I could hear was her murmuring voice, 'Oh! *Good* man! Oh! *Good* man!' and at that precise moment, and I swear that I am not exaggerating, at that *precise* moment, the great bell high in the dome of St Peter's began to strike midnight. Boom! Boom! Boom!, reverberating distantly far, far above us all. It was a quite extraordinary piece of theatre, and it was utterly of the moment. Presently she rose with supple grace and came through the barrier to join us. We stood in silence with the muffled bell booming, Edith with her head bowed in some kind of prayer, the light from the single bulbs hanging gaunt hoops beneath our eyes, the candle-shadows dancing among the flowers on the tomb and the whitewashed walls. A very strange gathering. And she a staunch Christian Scientist. V. odd.

Clambering up the twisting stairs, carrying her coat, I asked her what she would do with the carnation which she had been given. 'Treasure it,' she said between gasps. (It really *was* a climb.) 'I shall stick it in a very heavy book, which I have at home, and keep it there. For all eternity.'

It was a strange half hour, I must admit. The Chief of All the Police in Rome seemed as much moved as I was. He had, of course, watched Edith doing her 'pieces' in the church earlier and although he couldn't understand a word, he could see, he could hear, and the utter beauty of the vision, with that soaring lark-like voice sweeping up into the silent dome, had the most profound effect on us all. I truly don't think that Edith realised her impact at that time, she was so completely lost in the glory of the words which she had to say, and the splendour of that enormous, echoing, empty, basilica. A fusion of sheer physical beauty and sound ... which sprang tears to the eye.

There.

A long letter this, I hope that it has not bored you, but I felt I should write to you instantly while all was fresh in my mind, it was a cherished moment of which you share a tiny part, ill-written it may well be, but it *is* immediate.

Have you read the date at the head of this letter? Do you realise that we have hit a new decade together? We are now in the seventies, an odd feeling, but we have made it, girl. What the hell lies ahead? The perennial wonder. Nothing that we can do, for everything is pre-ordained anyway, it'll all take place whatever we try to do. I'd be very happy for another decade as interesting, full, strange and varied and as full of love as the last. But perhaps that is too much to ask? My hand is still here for the holding, I haven't weakened. Visconti, Venice, Von Aschenbach, and perhaps, *perhaps*, a new life in France. Who can say for certain?

Remember a lady called Jeanette MacDonald? She sang, rather badly, with tears in her eyes all through the thirties ... In something called *Monte Carlo*, sitting with her back to the engine, she sang blithely, to a fast moving landscape outside her compartment, 'Beyond the blue horizon/Awaits a wonderful day/Goodbye to all that bores me . . .' and etc., etc. That's rather how I feel this morning. We'll see. We'll see!

A happy, happy, new decade – hand quite steady. And *firm*.

EPILOGUE

Alas! My 'hand' was not always as available in the two years which followed into the new decade: or firm.

My life, very subtly, began to alter. Although I wrote as often as I could, it was not as often as I should, and very gradually, almost imperceptibly, we grew a little apart. It was, I suppose, inevitable.

Once I had removed myself from England and become totally immersed, as I did, in *Death in Venice*, there was little time for anything but Von Aschenbach and a demanding Visconti. I spent long days totally alone, preserving the strange creature (Von Aschenbach) who had, quite literally, 'taken me over'. He was a peevish fellow, and brooked no departure from his fastidious, monk-like life. I accepted this quite willingly, but it was hard on Mrs X, who wrote constantly and received, at best, a handful of postcards and, on rare occasions, a straggly, ill-written letter. She understood, of course: she *had* been warned; but it happened at a time when she needed me most, and I fear that I defaulted.

Moving to France gave me a little more freedom and life, though I was so immersed in restoring the house, pruning and digging, mending septic tanks and hacking out a potager from the limestone shale that there was little enough time for the hand which I had always promised to hold out to her in her pain and sadness. I did try very hard, but the torrent of cards and letters became merely a brook in the end, although she never failed, on any single day, to write. My 'hand', as it happened, was caked in mud, cut by thorns, cracked with frost, and corned by scythes, but I tried.

On March 21st 1971, in part of a letter which remains from her, she wrote:

... A phrase in your last letter set me thinking about marriage. From all that I see and hear ... it's for the birds.

For all our ridiculous 'carnet de famille' Robert [her husband of many years] and I never were nor felt married. It was a coup de foudre, which is apparently extremely rare ... that Platonic half-atom encountering its other half in the whirling universe ... a felicitous and perfect passionate fusion. Natural, inevitable. If you've experienced it, you *know*. If not, impossible to convey. It flowered in an ideal ambience ... leisure, ability to gratify every fleeting whim, isolation from people, a walled garden with Gloire de Dijon roses and espaliered fruit trees, and our devoted housekeeper, Marthe ... 'Ah, Madame, l'amour ... que c'est du bon dieu ça.'

But nothing lasts for ever, and you already know how grim were the seven years of severance. One found a foothold. Scars formed. One was thankful to be a vacuum, and rejected all human relationships lest one should ever F E E L again.

All the rest you know, my patient darling ... how reluctantly one was seduced, after all the frozen years, into an utterly fresh and joyous emotional involvement. The glacier thawing under untold heart's kindness, pouring, unasked, probably unwanted, but somehow understood, towards the owner of The House.

On February 24th Robert died. I hadn't seen him in twenty years, I was always prepared for the eventuality ... knowing that there could be no more grief. Oddly enough, I felt as though I had been kicked; and tried to laugh at myself and to reason. But mind over matter is a nice *theory*. The 'banjo' rebelled, the muscles ached. Probably a virus, so I went to the doctor. Blood pressure soaring, nothing else wrong. 'It looks like severe emotional shock with muscular tensions. Have you had a shock recently?' So I told him, adding, 'But that was weeks ago.' He laughed. 'Never can tell what the subconscious will do.' Perhaps.

Anyhow. That's what knocked me adrift. You are still so close to your own loss [the death from agonising cancer of Robin Fox, my agent and my friend] that you probably know how the memories come flooding in, the happier they are, the worse the pain. The guilt that one is still living, and for me the bleakness of not being needed by anyone.

It is hard to learn that aloneness is not an absolute term, but a relative one. So: continue to ridicule me as I try to ridicule myself. You must know how difficult it is to face finality with a sense of humour. My immediate instinct was to write to you. But I pictured you happy in your garden, or on the land and didn't want to bother you. I wish that I had your outlet for tears!

Here there wasn't a soul to speak to, and I suppose that, au fond, man is a social animal and needs a certain amount of communication. Else why was he endowed with speech.

These are stupid words. All I know is that I love you and that you will manage to understand 'the underside of the leaf'.

Health and happiness to you, darling!

One year later, almost to the date, I find another letter, or fragment of, which proves that, even with so much work on hand, for my part, and even without the energy needed to write *daily* (I had stopped this by now, and wrote a long sort of bulletin once a week, being no longer spurred by romantic emotion), we stayed closely in touch nevertheless. This fragment (I have the first page only) is dated March 20th '72 and things don't seem to be really any different from how they have been for years. She writes:

By the way, I do agree that our affaire is by far the best! If I should ever see you I am sure that all the pent-up devotion for you would burst forth in a rash worse than any measles! But I take exception to your comment that we reveal only 'the most delicious parts of us'. The very WORST of me has been poured forth to you, as you have so often complained: 'whimpering' and etc. ... The beauty of this is that we don't have the daily 'wear and tear' of rubbing along together day after mundane day with all of Nanny's potential 'nasties'. It's a bit Keats ... 'For ever panting and forever young' and, to paraphrase: 'He cannot fade, though thou has not thy bliss/ Forever wilt thou love, and he be fair.' Impossible to really know someone as unfathomable as you, thank God! And there are many times when you are 'way off' about me! But a basic, mysterious 'rapport' does exist, thank Heaven. All the beauty in my life.

Damn words! It needs new minted iridescent shimmering ... what? flowers? to convey what I feel. Oh come on soppy girl, get on with a bit of Eddie Marsh, the war-time book and perhaps vieux jeu to you. But meant to cheer. No doubt you did not notice, but I took the letter-before-last down to the mailbox on my very own. Rather than have you wait extra days. My knees almost buckled under me, but, by Golly, I made it.

Saw some snowdrops, and the little green noses of croci and hyacinths poking out. Spring?

Oh ... shall I now have to 'blue' my hair, to live up to your image of an American Tourist? It is startling to suddenly see white instead of black! Lucky that I don't 'live on my looks' and can laugh at this curious and quite unexpected transformation.

This is a birthday letter, so cup my love in your hands for a moment (would burn if held too long!), and then toss it over the terrace or spit on it if you will. It will, whatever you do with it, bless you for eternity ...

For a month after this, she wrote as constantly as ever, but there was a sense of distress in her letters which had never been there before. She was acutely worried as to what she should do with 'the letters'. After all, we had been writing to each other since 1967 every day, practically, at least on her side, on mine less as I became more and more involved with my brave new world in France. To my bitter regret I wrote, on April 21st '72, a cruel and thoughtless postcard.

Up to my eyes with work. Don't give a damn to whom you leave my ruddy letters. Yale, Harvard or the British Museum, or try St Pancras, why not? Do as you like, if it makes you feel better, I really do not care. Will write when I am sorted out.

The card, later returned to me with all the rest of my letters, was of the local village church and churchyard. She received it on the morning of the day that she died, and filed it, as she had done with all the rest, neatly in a folder with the exact date and time of its arrival and wrote the following:

April 28th 1972

Darling, your April 21st starling arrived this morning, and brought a measure of relief, bless you! Ever since your 'black-mail' came, I've been in an indigo depression, too deep to write, and living on sedatives to keep the blood pressure from doing a fandango.

... the LETTERS should be published ... they are so full of glorious writing! But I never know when you are being tongue-in-cheek. My death would be the appropriate moment. And I feel that you should edit them. I can delete some of the 'obscenities', but I have no way of judging what episodes you would want omitted. Only you know that. Also, I have a *horror* of exploiting your name, fame and generosity. Surely, you can understand that! I've been mulling and mulling over the whole idea ... yes, I thought of the British Museum ... also wondered if there were some London or Liverpool archive where you would prefer to have them. I do appreciate your modesty, but it is unwarranted.

What I cannot bear equably is a malentendu between us!

I haven't been feeling at all well lately ... should go to the doctor, but am trying to hold out until my next check-up in May. Hate to go.

Perhaps some wet cold day, when the mistral is blowing, you will feel like 'talking' again ... but by then you will no doubt be on location, and far too occupied. I *wish* you could know what your LETTERS mean to me ... when you are in the mood and have leisure! I have been going through some of the 1967–68 ones, and they improve with age. I wish you would be franker with me about their disposal ... publishing, etc. I'm shaking as I write this, so will reach for a sedative, and close, since you are too busy even to read nonsense.

Hope you are having fine weather and enjoying your garden. Here, spring seems to appear momentarily, and then drop back to 30°.

Except for the LETTER problem, merely a bluejay.

Oh, I saw Penelope Mortimer's *The Pumpkin Eaters* [sic], scripted, I believe, by Pinter (anyhow, he was affiliated with it). Drastically and badly cut for TV, and extremely poor. Too bad. *New York Times* comment 'Pinter pens a pickle' ... whatever that may mean.

If this bluejay sounds 'unnatural', please blame it on ill-health – *not* a dearth of love.

Before I received this there was a bleak cable on May 2nd which stated: 'Regret Mrs X died of heart attack Friday night.' I was signed with an unknown name. Some days later, when the grief was less intense and I was going about my chores on the land, a letter arrived which will end this little saga pretty well. There is nothing more to say after all.

7389 Amalfi Street
N.Y.

May 19th 1972

Dear Sir:

We have both lost a very good friend.

I hope that you will not think me presumptuous in writing to you.

I only wish to thank you for being so kind to my Madam, Mrs X.

She looked forward to your letters as she enjoyed them so much, when you had the House (in England) she relived her pleasure in living there. She sure loved it.

I threatened many times to write and tell you and to thank you, she seemed pleased.

You will be happy to know that in her last few days she was so happy because of all your letters.

Again, thank you for giving her so much pleasure.

God bless you always.

Anna C. Paulaka
Her friend and her maid

INDEX